AF576705

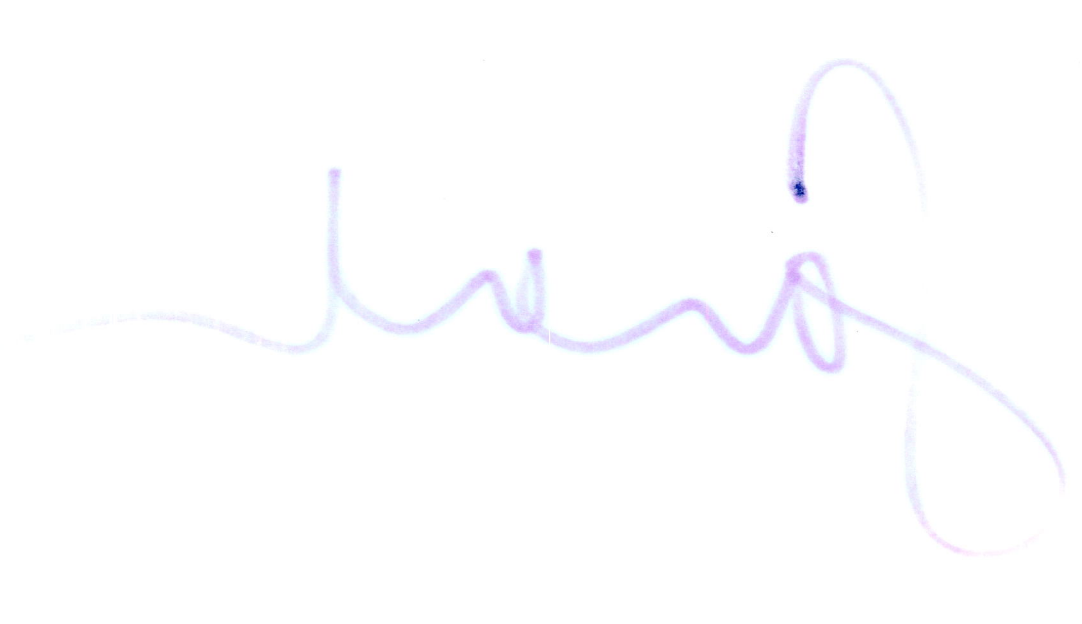

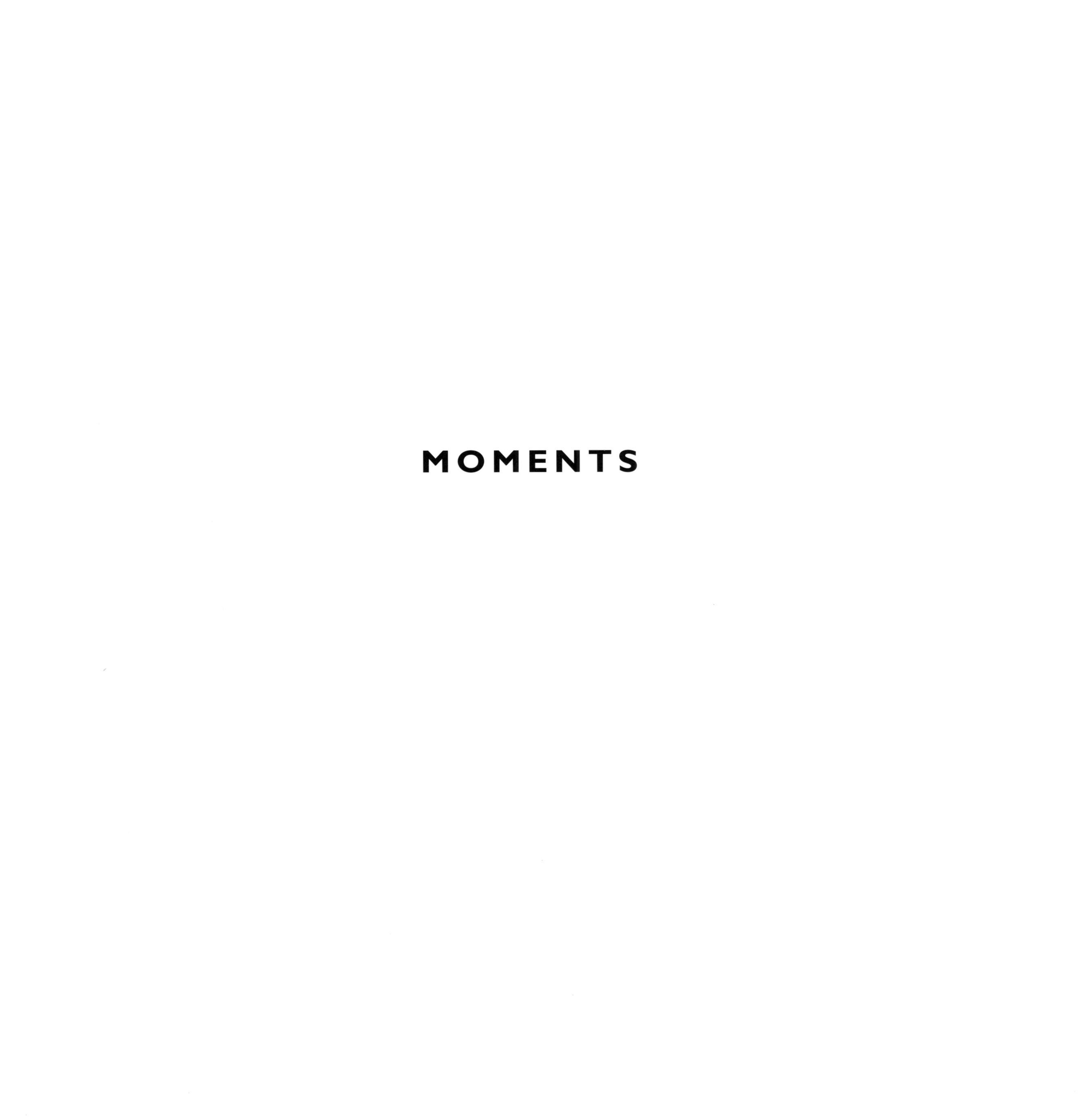

MOMENTS

MOMENTS

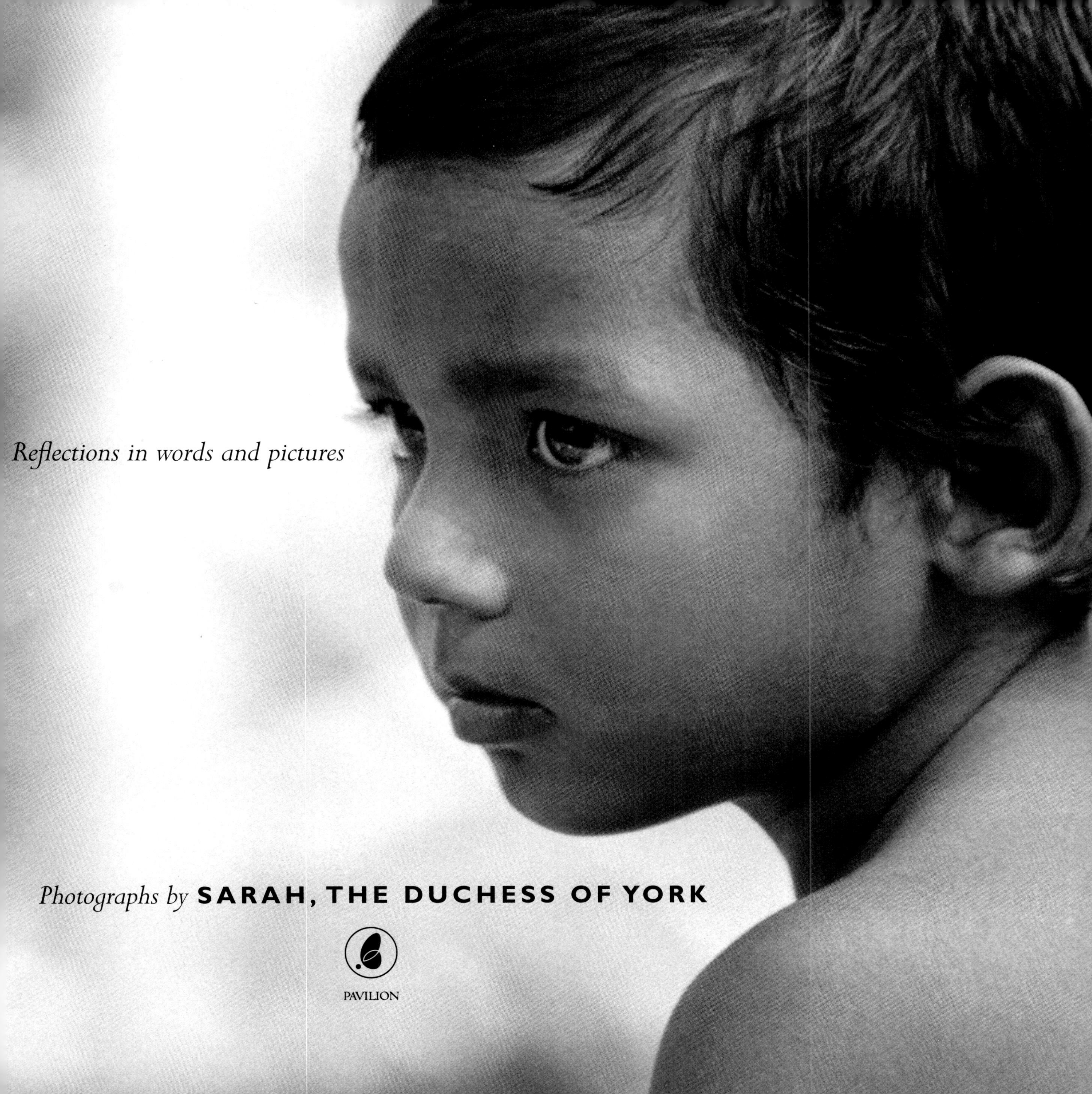

Reflections in words and pictures

Photographs by **SARAH, THE DUCHESS OF YORK**

PAVILION

Dearest MDB – thank you for teaching me to look at life with clear eyes and a strong heart. I cherish your golden soul and your friendship is truly a blessing which makes my world complete... You are unique.

Ann-Louise Dyer – your stars have opened my eyes to the light and shown me a different world.
Sarah

First published in Great Britain in 2003 by Pavilion Books
A member of Chrysalis Books plc
64 Brewery Road
London N7 9NT
www.chrysalisbooks.co.uk

ISBN 1 86205 573 4

10 9 8 7 6 5 4 3 2 1

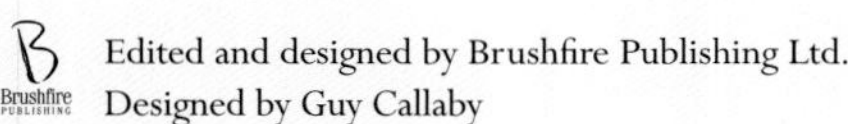

Edited and designed by Brushfire Publishing Ltd.
Designed by Guy Callaby

A CIP catalogue record for this book is available from the British Library

Printed in Singapore by Imago

ACKNOWLEDGEMENTS
The Publishers are grateful for permission to reproduce copyright material. Whilst every reasonable effort has been made to trace copyright holders, the publishers would be pleased to hear from any not acknowledged.

FOREWORD

I never intended on being a photographer. I was self-taught. I picked up a camera quite accidentally and unintentionally began interpreting familiar faces and surroundings. I was attracted to the Southern California elements: light, texture, form and the expanse from the sea to the desert. Through the camera I learned to express what I found in front of my eyes and was drawn to it. The resulting photographs conveyed my emotional bond to my environment. I was inspired and I enjoyed it immensely. I found my niche and never looked back.

Sarah is a visual enthusiast. She is uninhibited and goes for it. Her camera has become a welcome friend accompanying her on her travels. It has helped her realize and personally connect her intimate feelings, ranging from family to the planet. She is inspired and encouraged by what she sees and wants others to share in the pleasures of her moments.

I salute her earnest efforts and may she enjoy the process for many years to come.

Herb Ritts 2002

Herb Ritts was always a great source of inspiration and encouragement to me and I was truly honoured when he agreed to write the foreword to this book. His death in December 2002 has left an irreplaceable void in the world of photography and he will be greatly missed. He was an exceptional photographer and a wonderful friend.

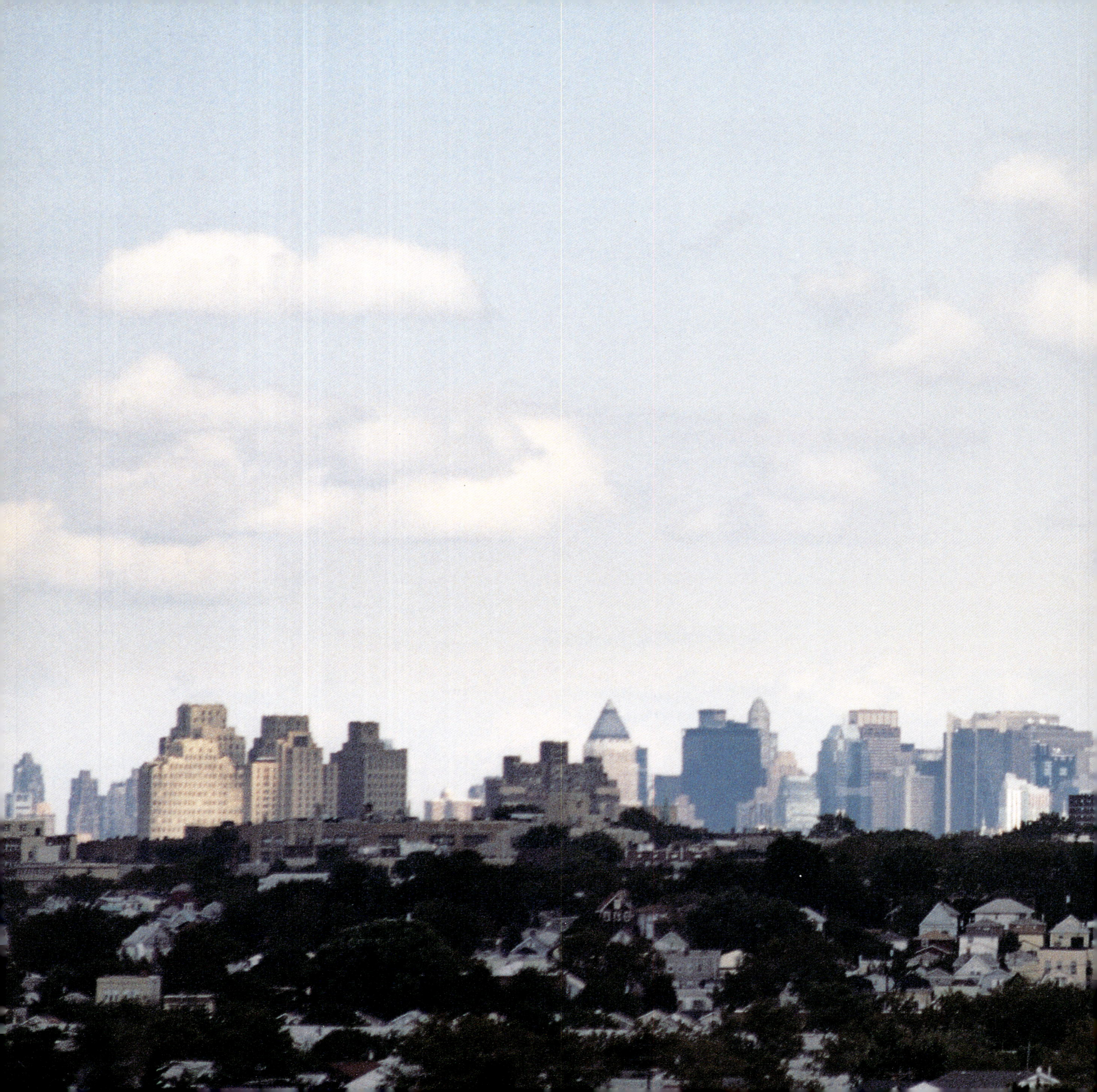

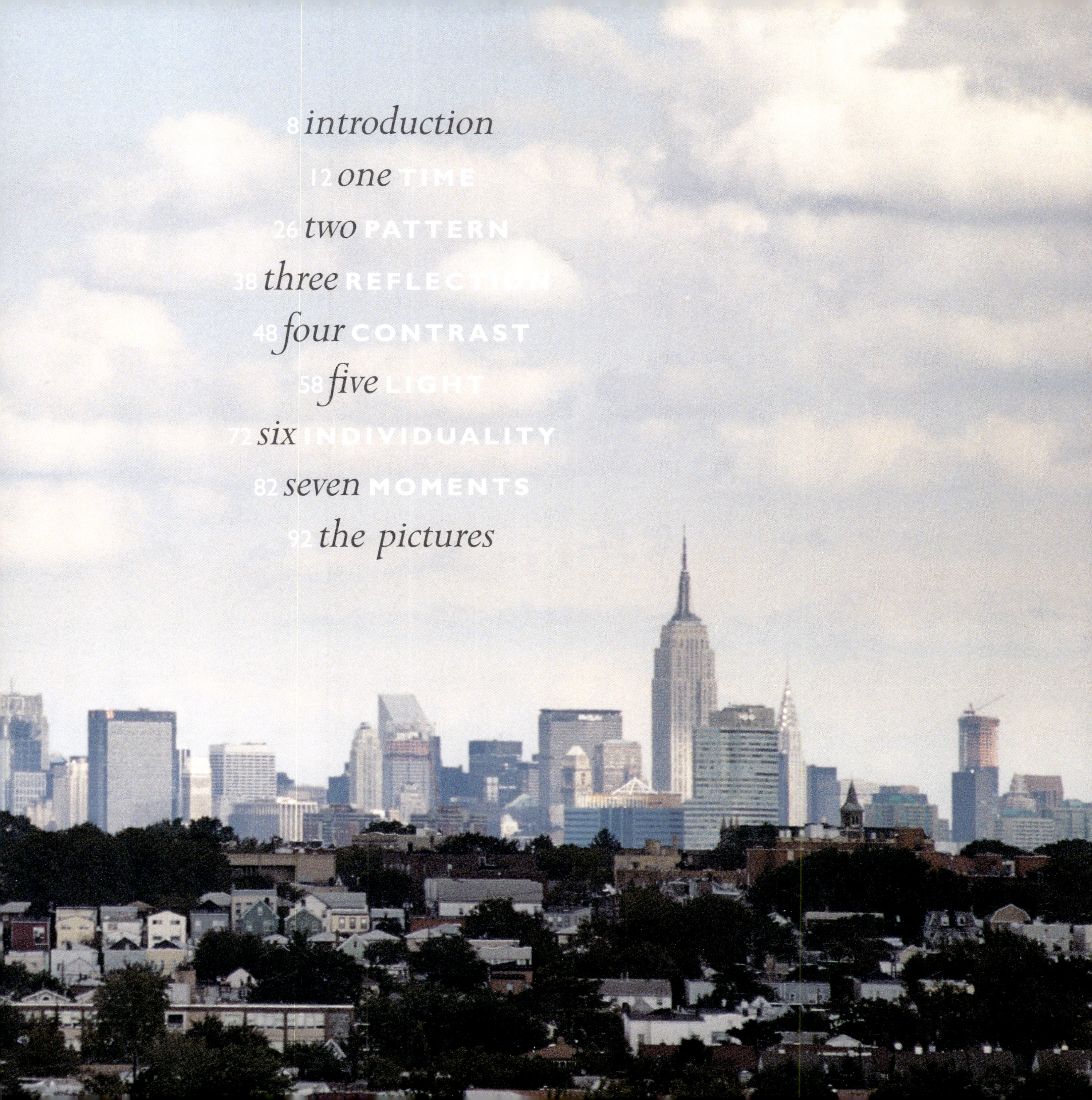

INTRODUCTION

For me, photography is a form of escapism. It is fascinating to look at life through the lens of a camera and then to capture the essence of the moment Sometimes, I hide behind my camera to avoid being in front of others! This book is a collection of some of my photographs, most of which I have coupled with some favourite quotes or fragments of literature, which have been a source of inspiration and comfort to me and I hope that you find some of these quotations as uplifting and energising as I do.

I first began to take photographs shortly after my eldest daughter, Beatrice, was born. My main aim then was to capture her ever-changing face as she grew so quickly from newborn to toddler to child, not only for my personal albums but for her too, so that in later life she could look back at snapshots of her childhood.

With the arrival of my second daughter, Eugenie, I found myself with a camera almost permanently around my neck. Time is so fleeting, and so precious, I cherish those early photographs dearly and I am so glad that I have such a comprehensive record of the girls' childhoods – their birthday parties, Christmas, horse riding, and other childhood activities.

The photograph of Andrew and Eugenie on pages 84 and 85, I hope, will be one for Eugenie to treasure when she is older. It captures that incredibly powerful feeling a parent has for a child and is a wonderful example of how deep those two people's feelings are for each other – it is probably my favourite photograph of them both.

I am undoubtedly, incredibly fortunate to have been in a position where I have been able to travel this world so extensively. As I became more confident with my camera, I started to experiment and examine the varying landscapes which I encountered on my journeys. I began, tentatively, to take shots of them and found that the results were exciting and gave me enormous pleasure. Due to the nature of my life, I tend to be permanently on the move and therefore believe that it is

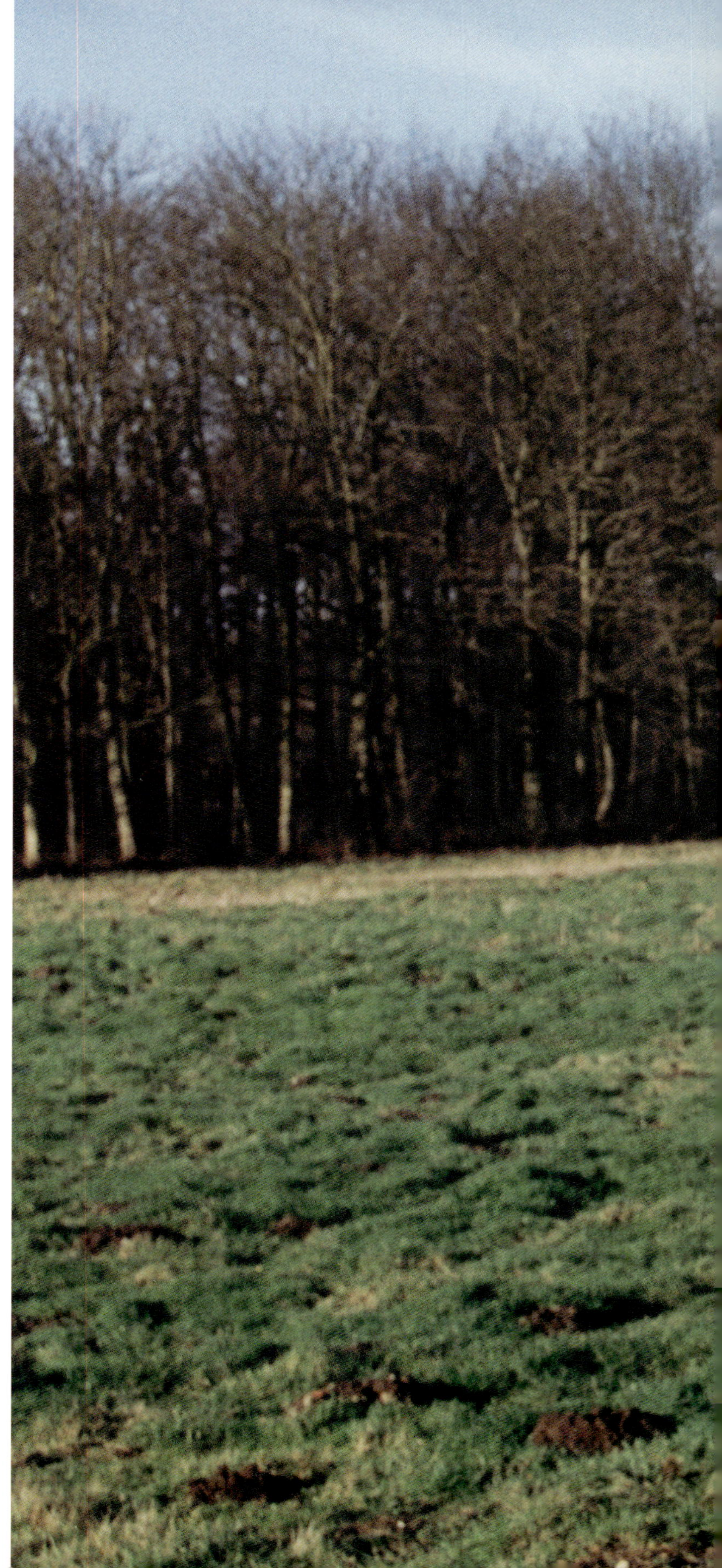

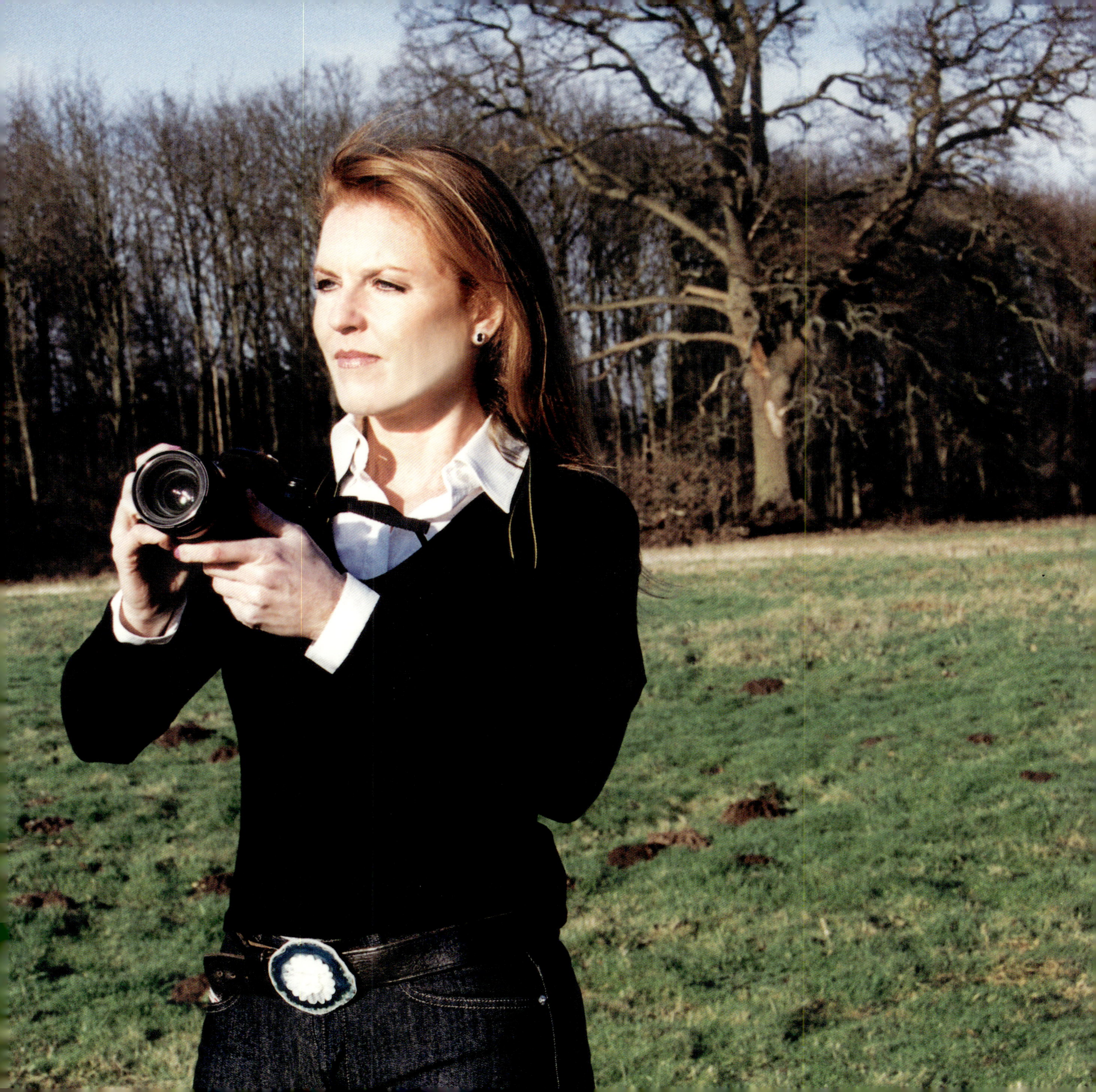

important, sometimes, just to stop and appreciate the beauty of the world in which we live.

To have the opportunity to stop, to stand still, to admire a vista and to shoot it is rewarding beyond belief. Not only does this then allow me to really open my eyes to the surroundings in which I find myself, but it also gives me a permanent reminder of those places which I have visited. I now have a pictorial travel journal, if you like, and all of my photographs are catalogued in albums. I always have a camera by my side and, whenever possible, I will take time out of a busy working schedule and start snapping – whether it be from a hotel room in middle America or from an aeroplane. One of the photographs of which I am most proud is on page 22 and was taken from a car whilst I was hurrying to a speaking engagement in New York.

In many of my landscapes I have tried to capture a feeling of solitude. Most of the time, I am surrounded by people and moving around the world at breakneck speed. Sometimes, I love to relish the feeling of being completely alone in the world and there is no greater place for such tranquillity and isolation than in Patagonia, Argentina. The landscape is so varied and always full of surprises, with magical sunsets and awe-inspiring vistas.

I am under no illusion that I will ever reach the ranks of the most talented photographers, but to have the chance to be creative on my own initiative is enough reward for me. I hope that, if like me, you are a keen amateur, you will leaf through this book and be encouraged to pick up your camera. Every day we are reminded how precious and short life is – yesterday is history and tomorrow is a mystery. Seize the opportunity, open your eyes, raise your camera to them and capture the moment!

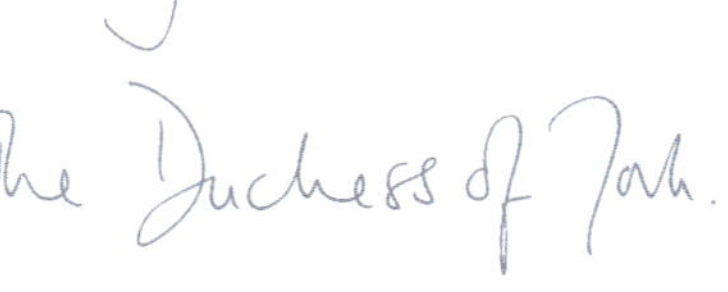

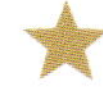

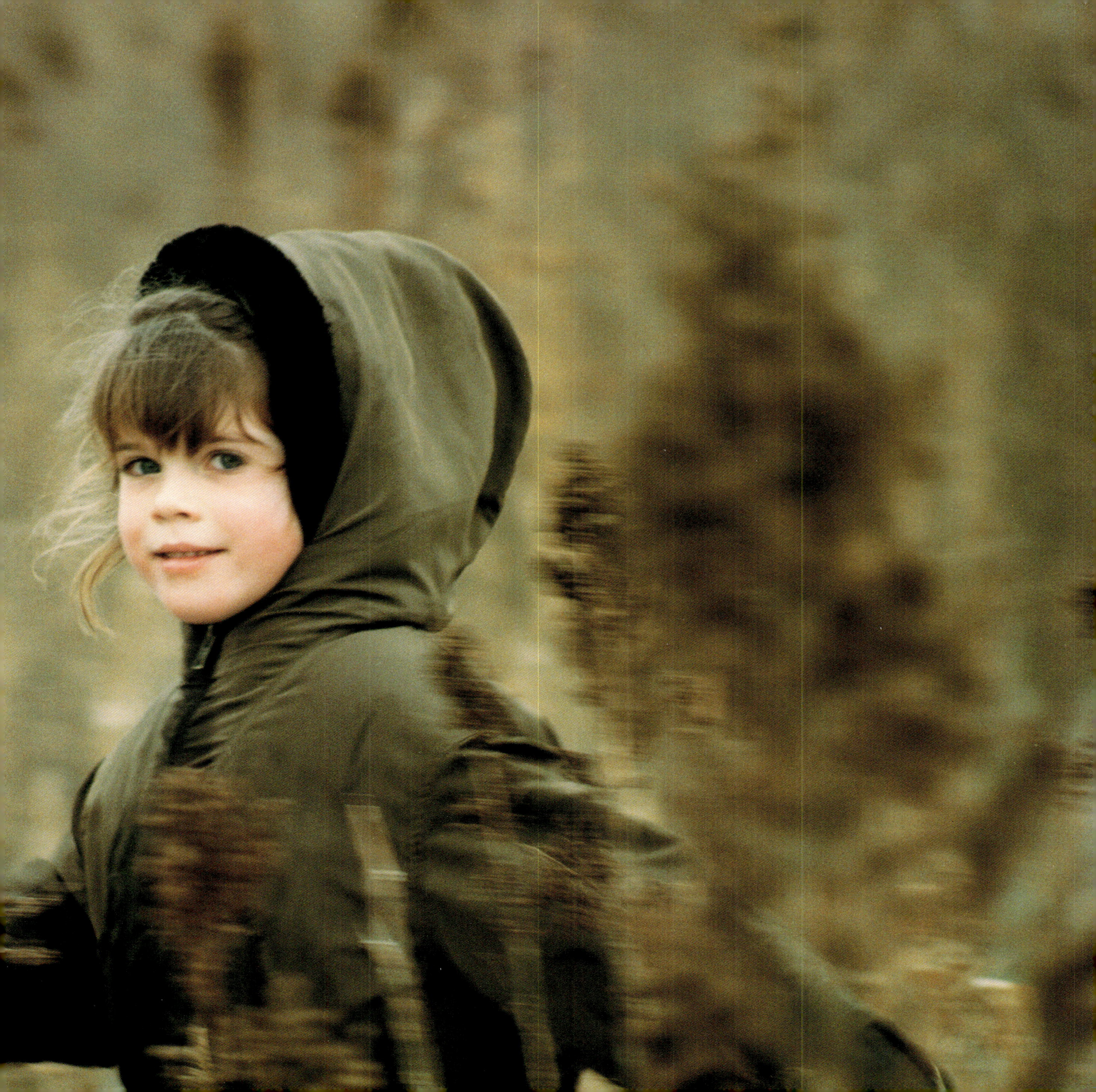

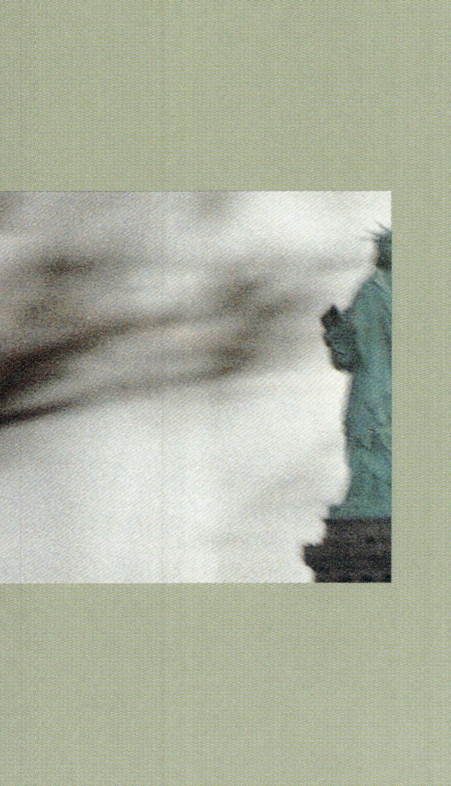

one TIME

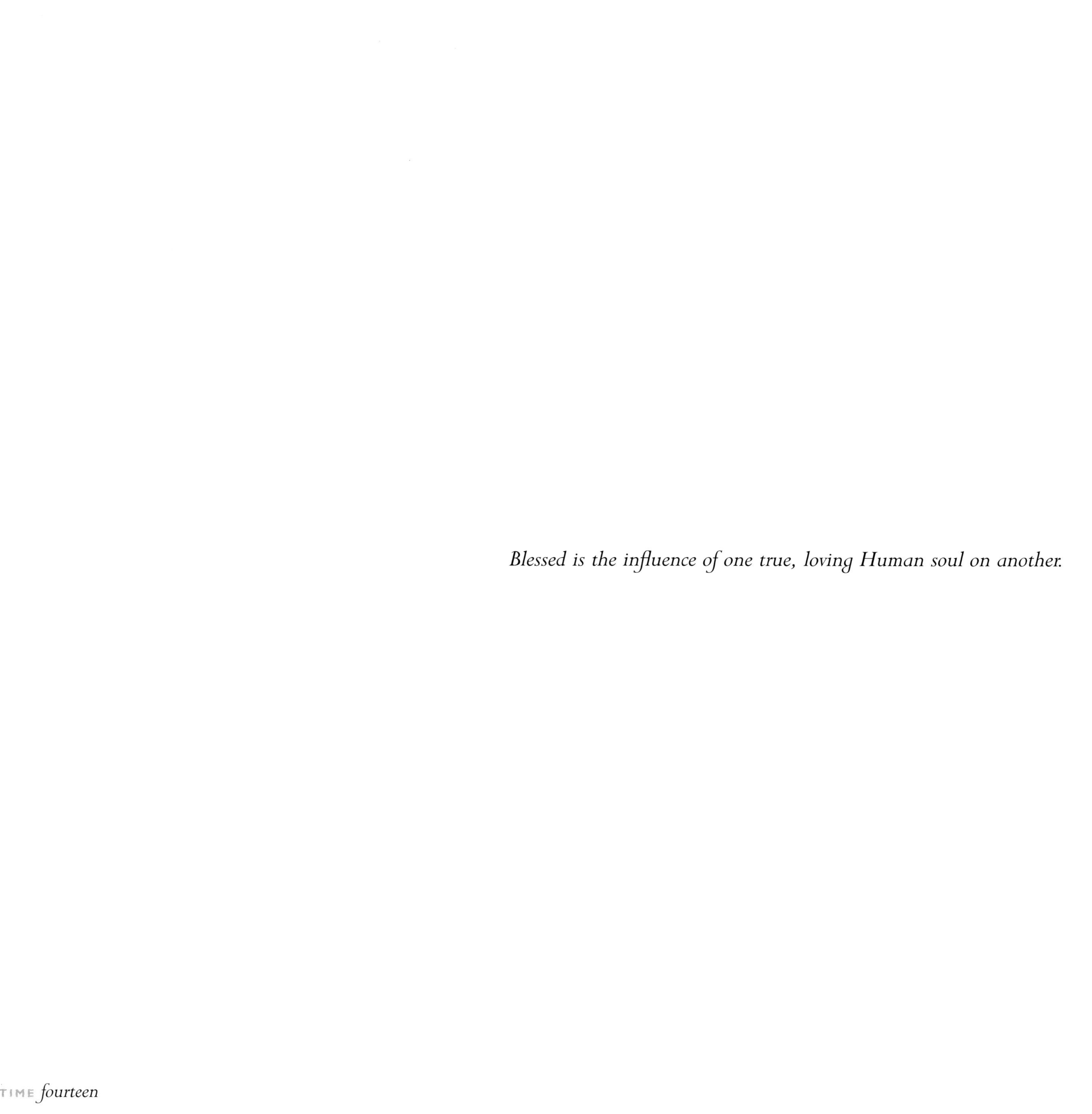

Blessed is the influence of one true, loving Human soul on another.

GEORGE ELIOT

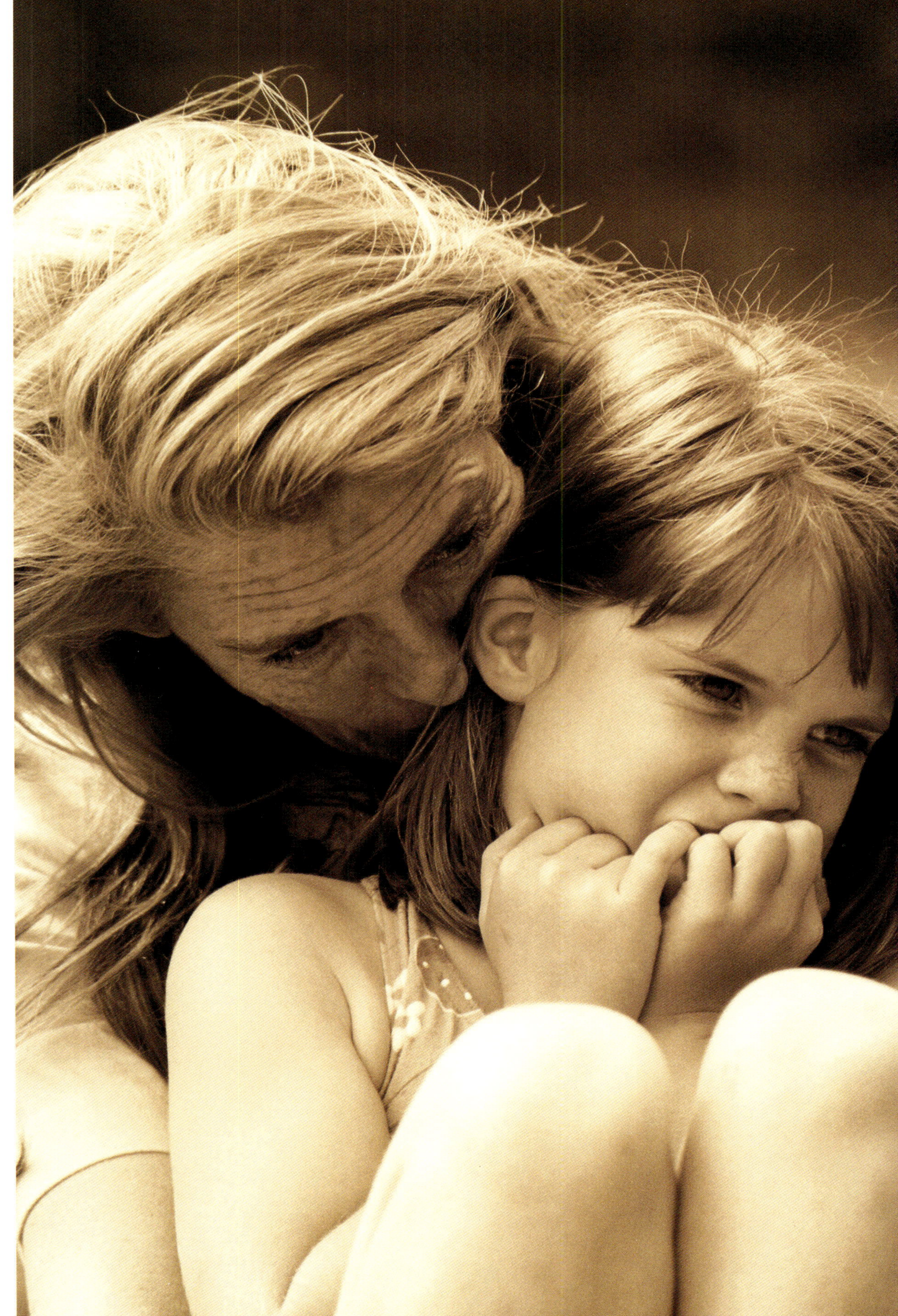

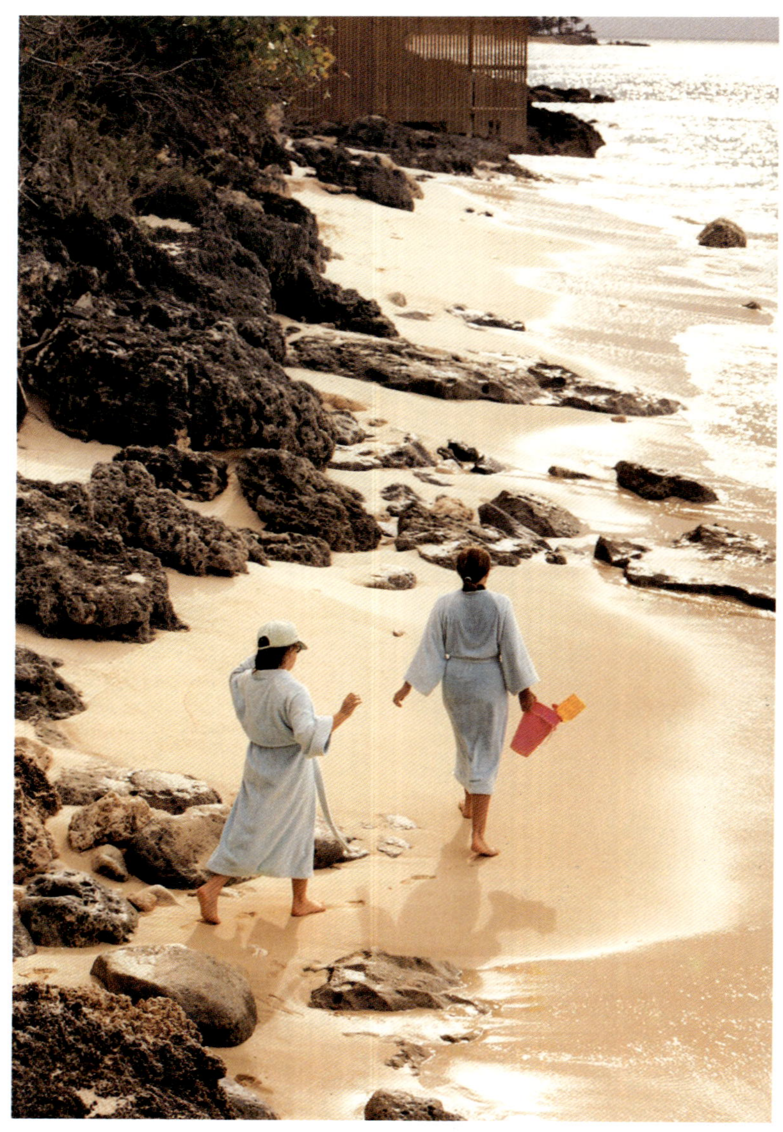

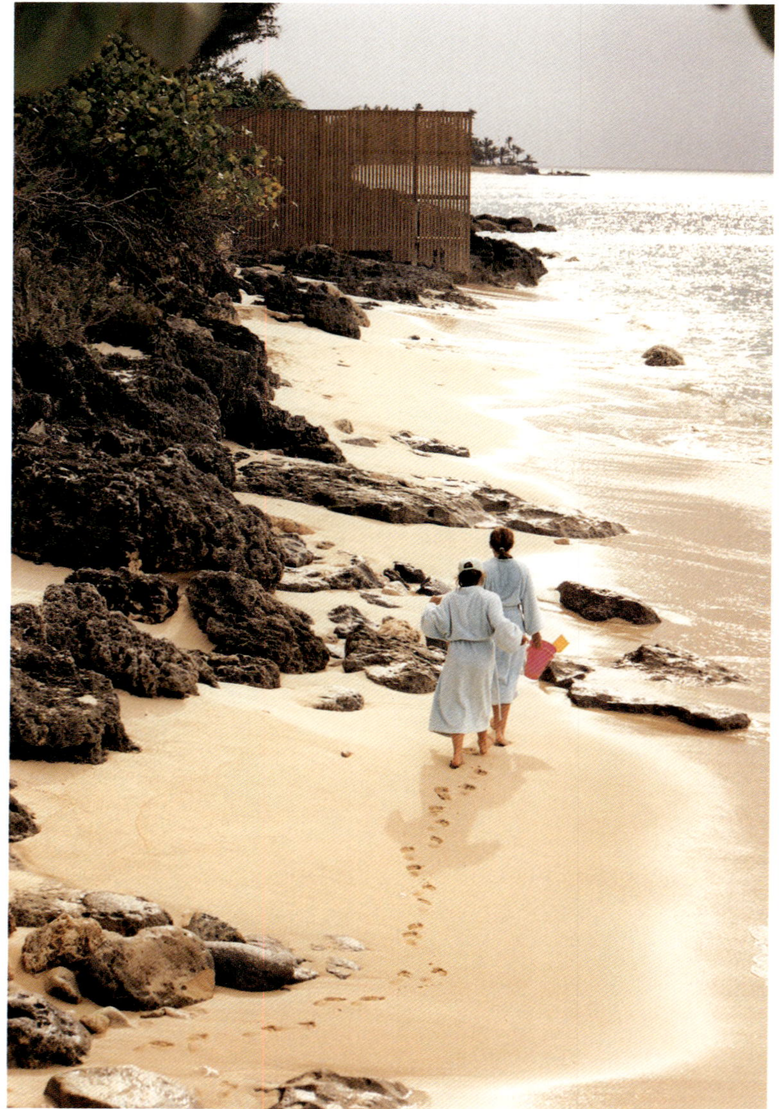

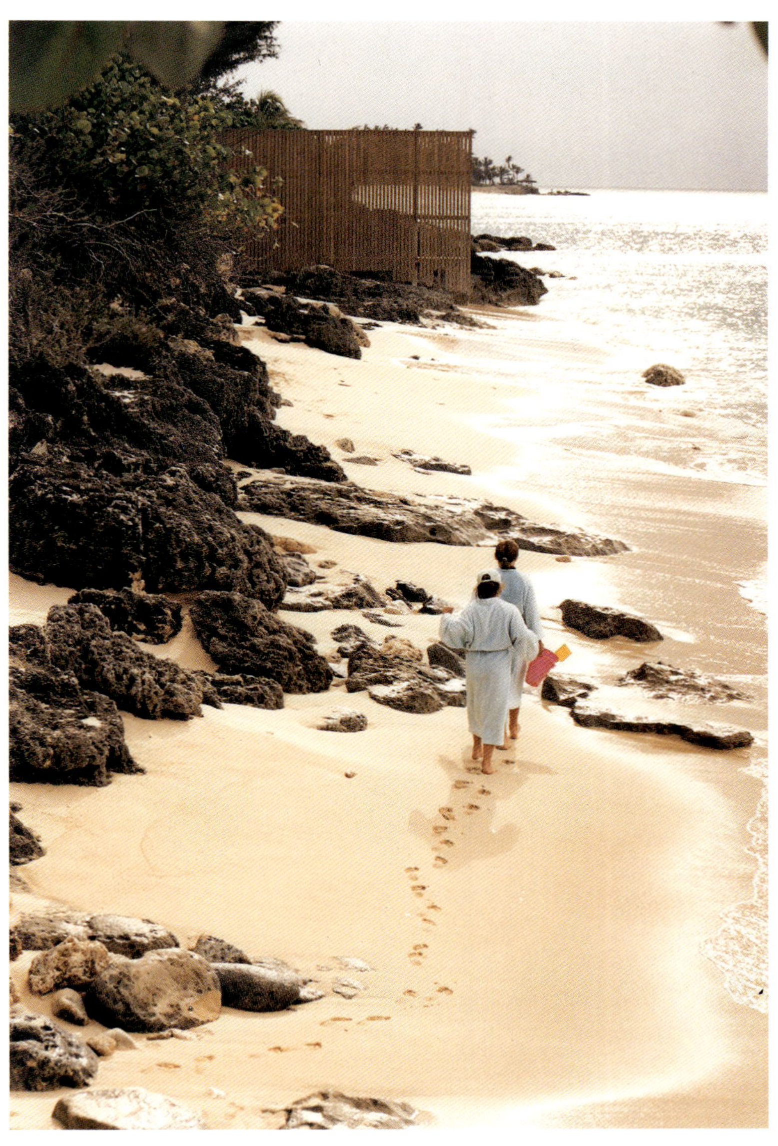

It took years for us to find our own pace,
to create a silence in which to hear only
the sound of our own footsteps and not feel
that the silence was a lonely emptiness.

POLLY DEVLIN

'SISTERS'

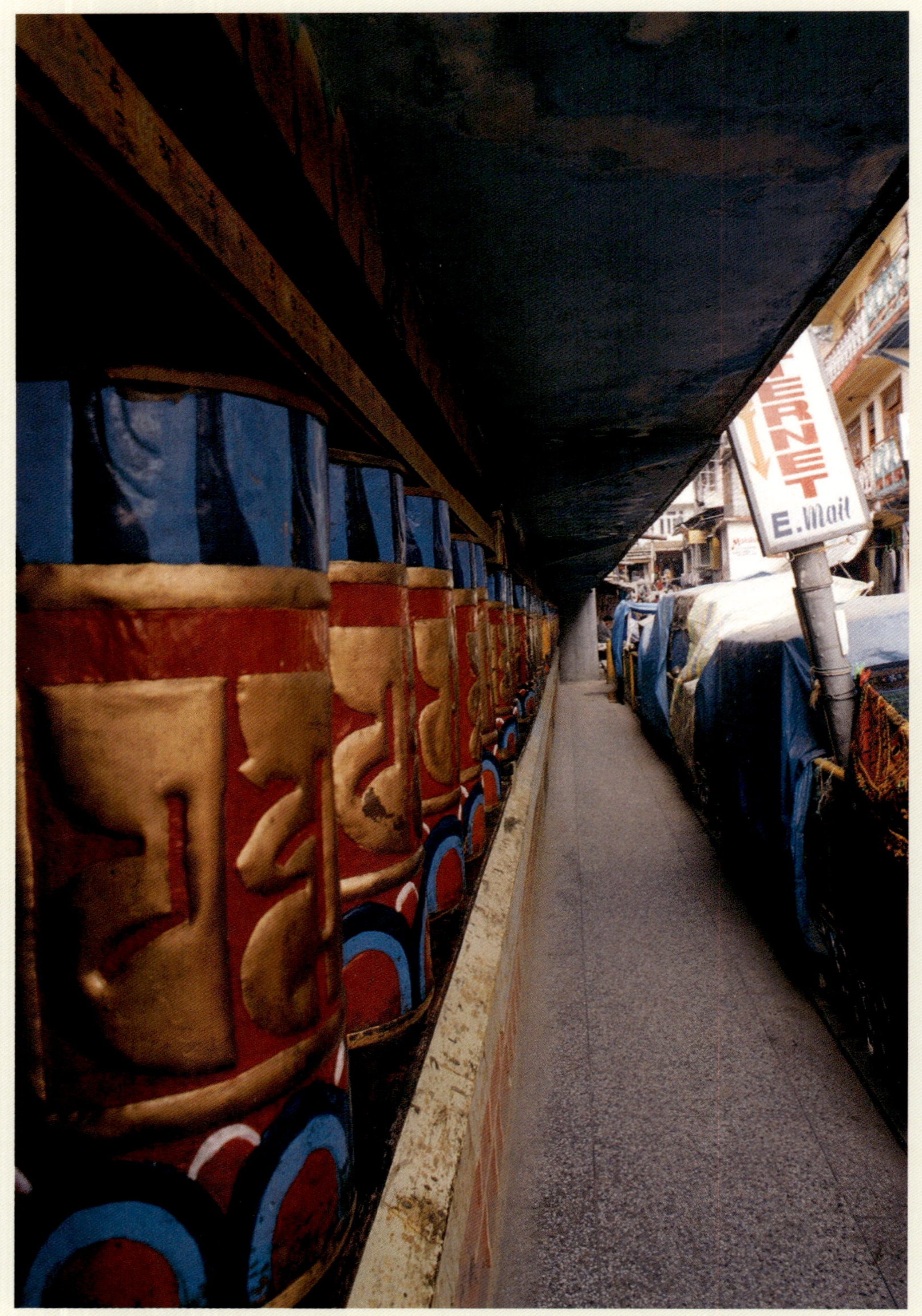
ERNET
E.Mail

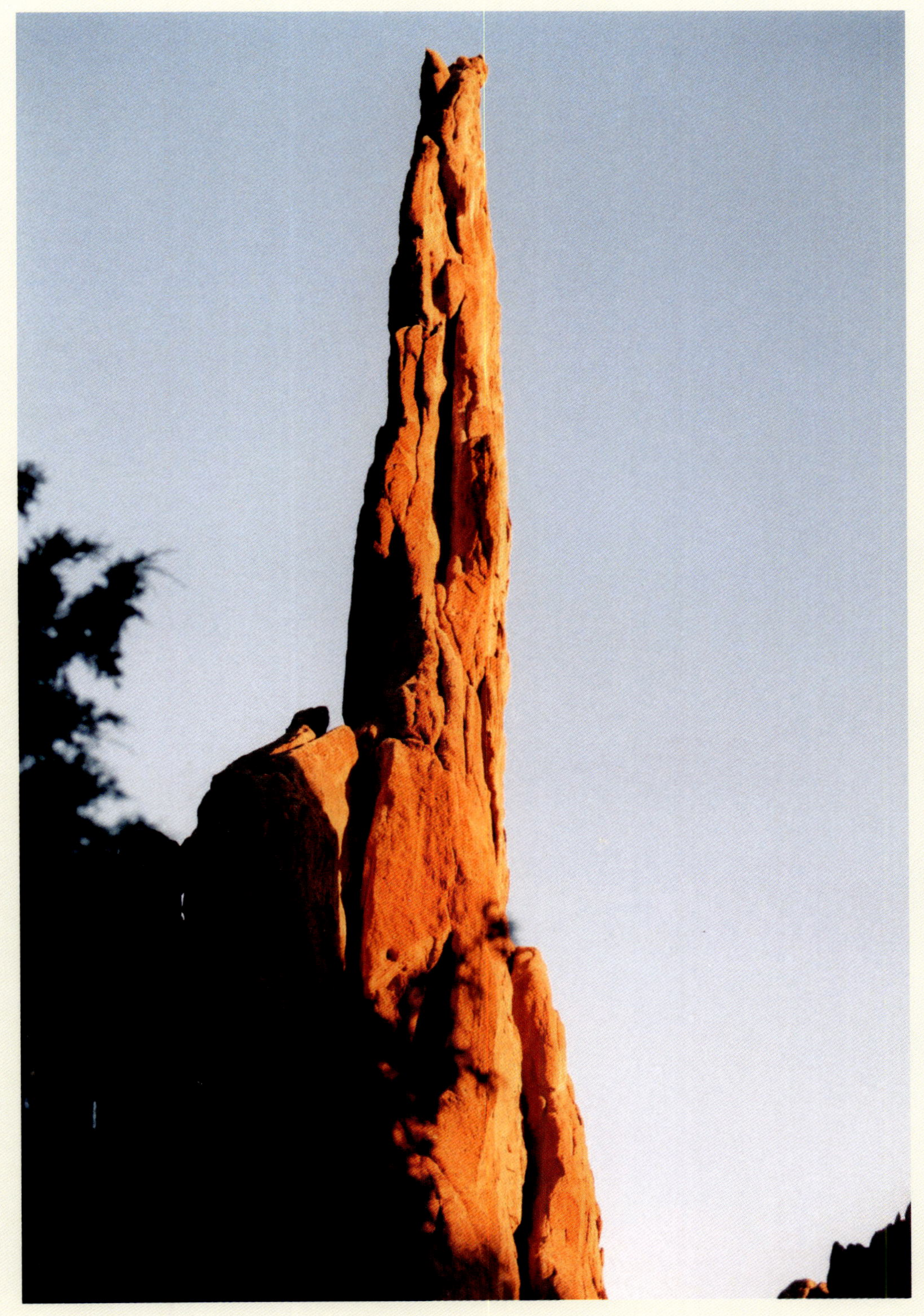

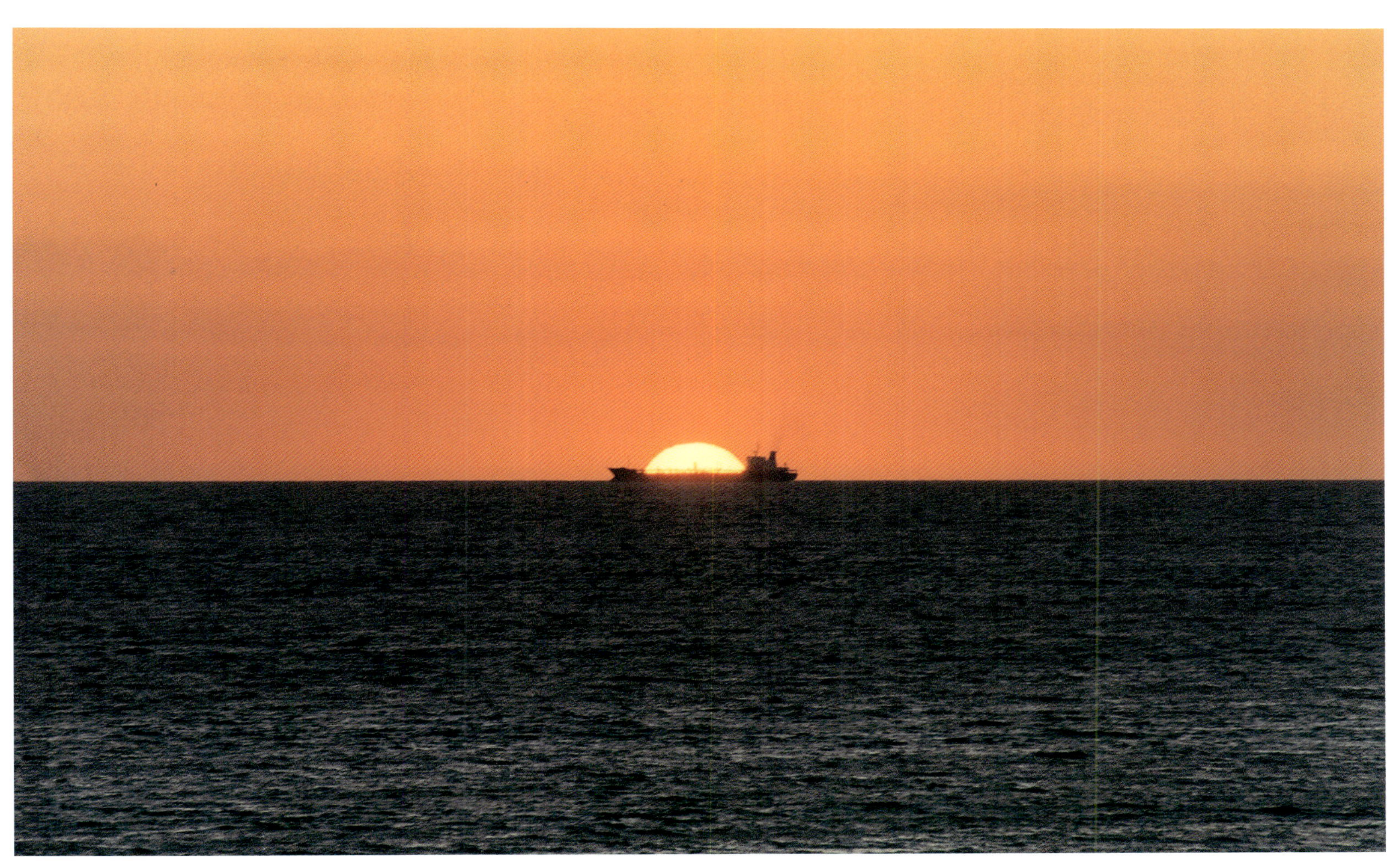

There is great happiness in not wanting,

In not being something,

In not going somewhere.

J. KRISHNAMURTI

We hold these **TRUTHS**
to be **SACRED** *and*
UNDENIABLE; *that all*
men are created **EQUAL**
and **INDEPENDENT**, *that*
from that equal
creation they derive
RIGHTS *inherent and*
inalienable, among
which are the
preservation of **LIFE**,
and **LIBERTY**, *and the*
pursuit of **HAPPINESS**.

THOMAS JEFFERSON

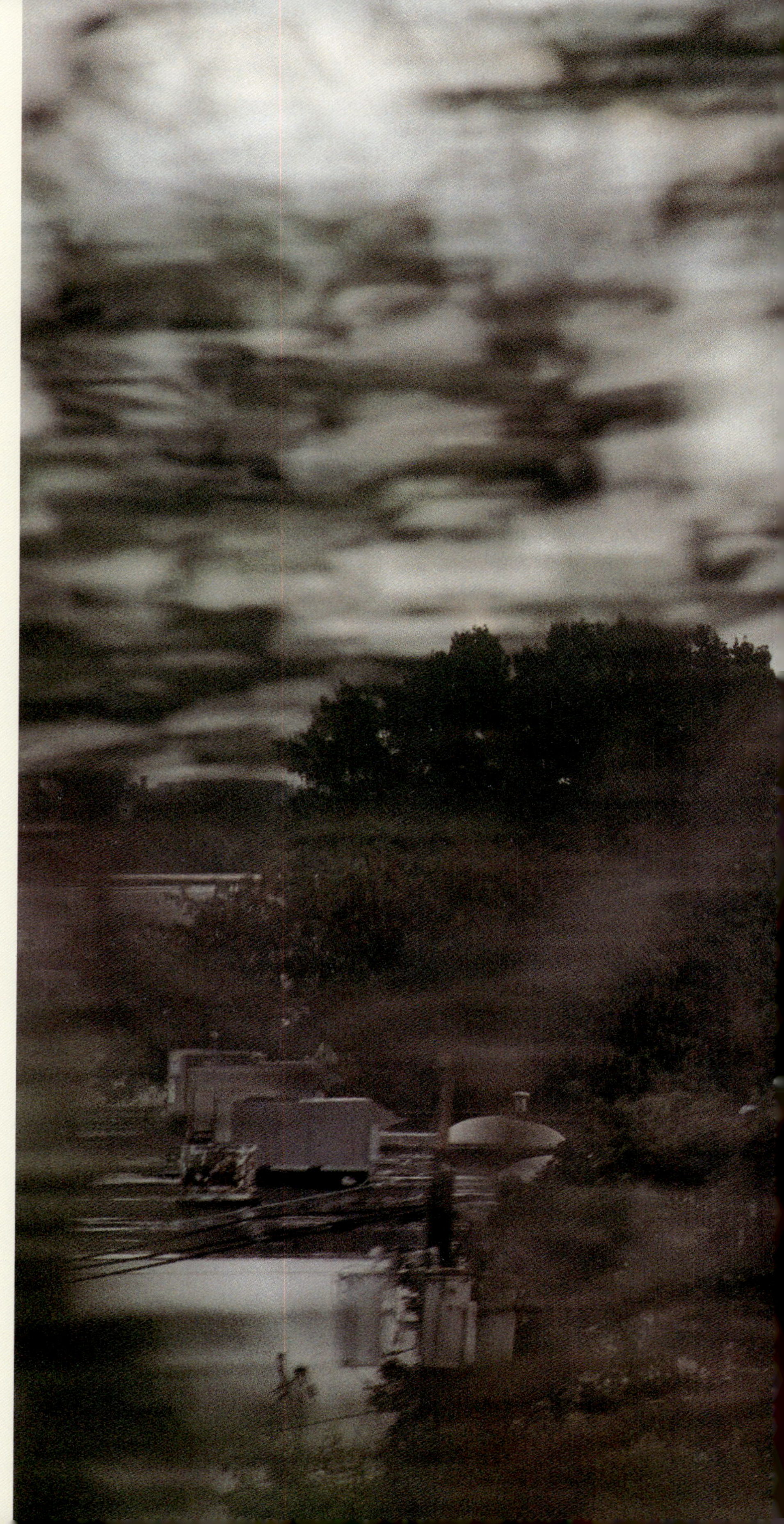

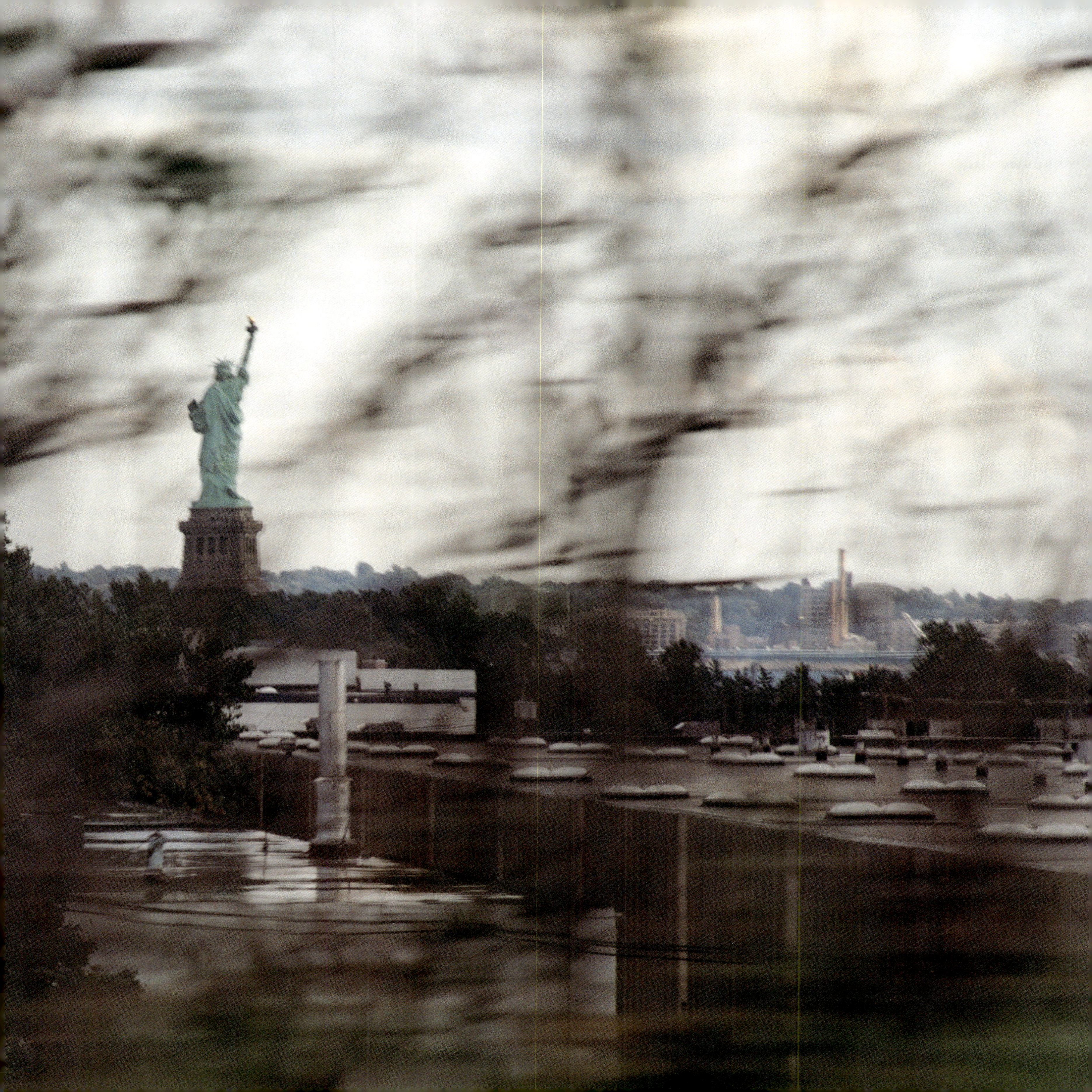

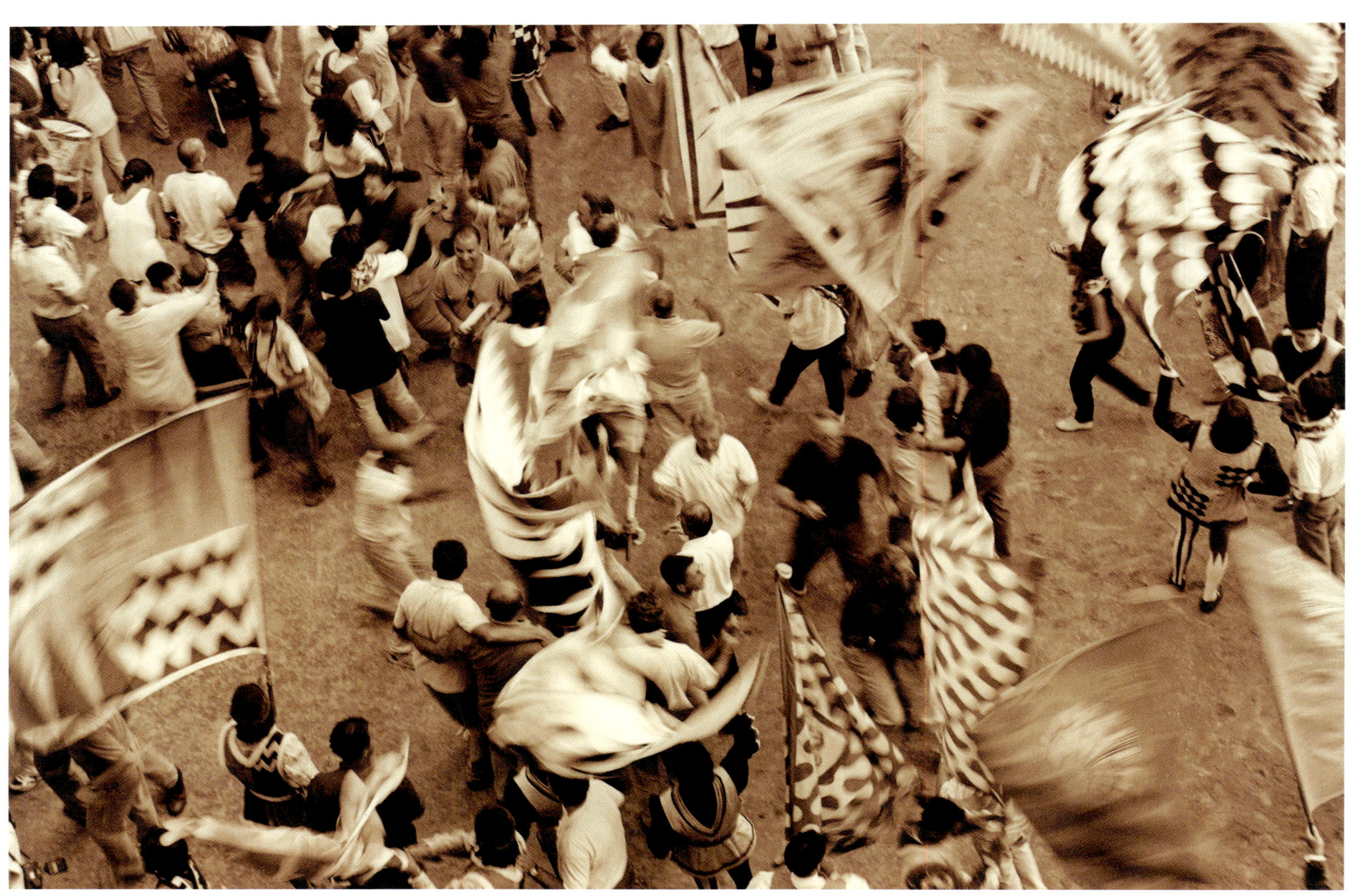

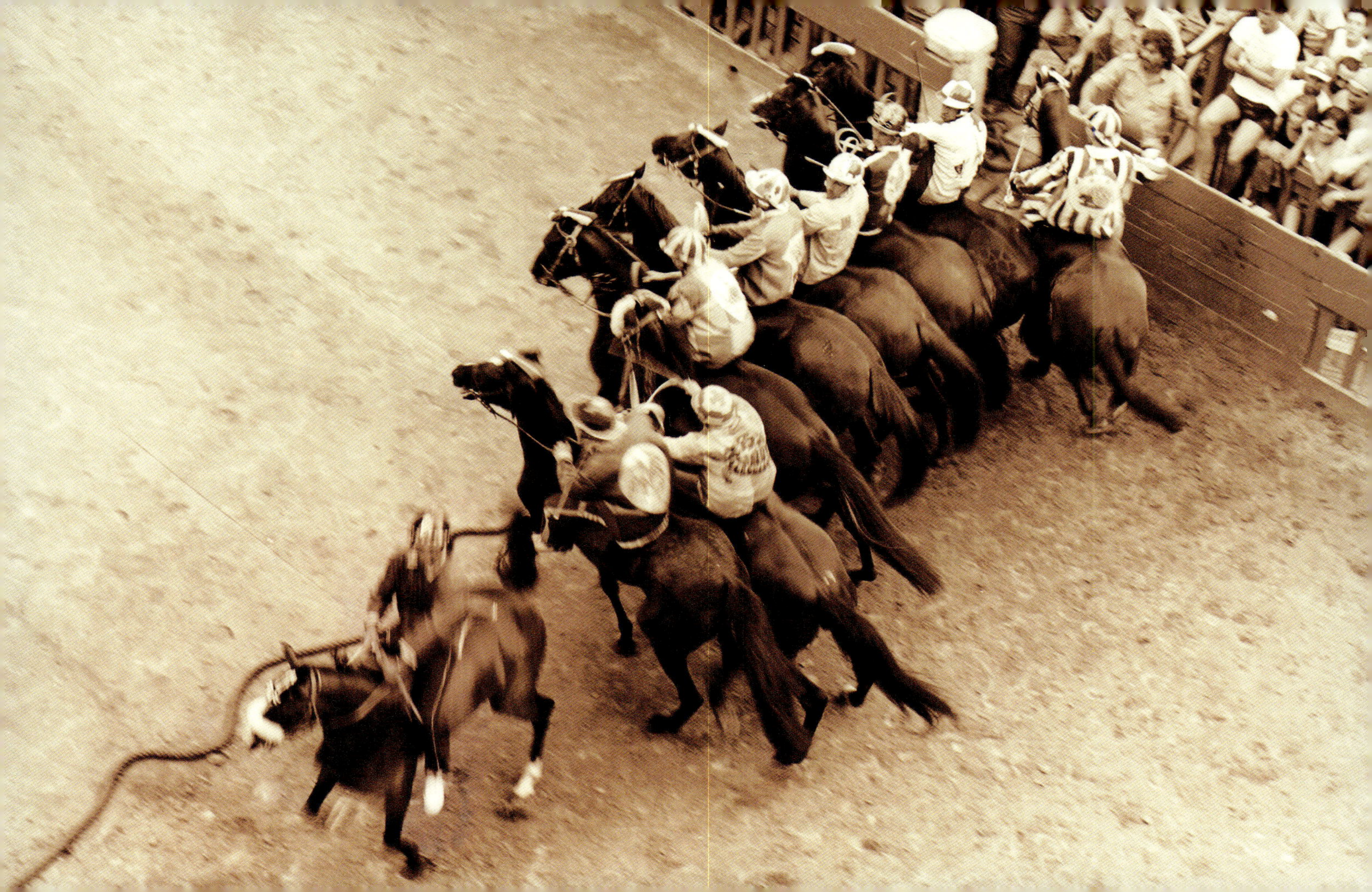

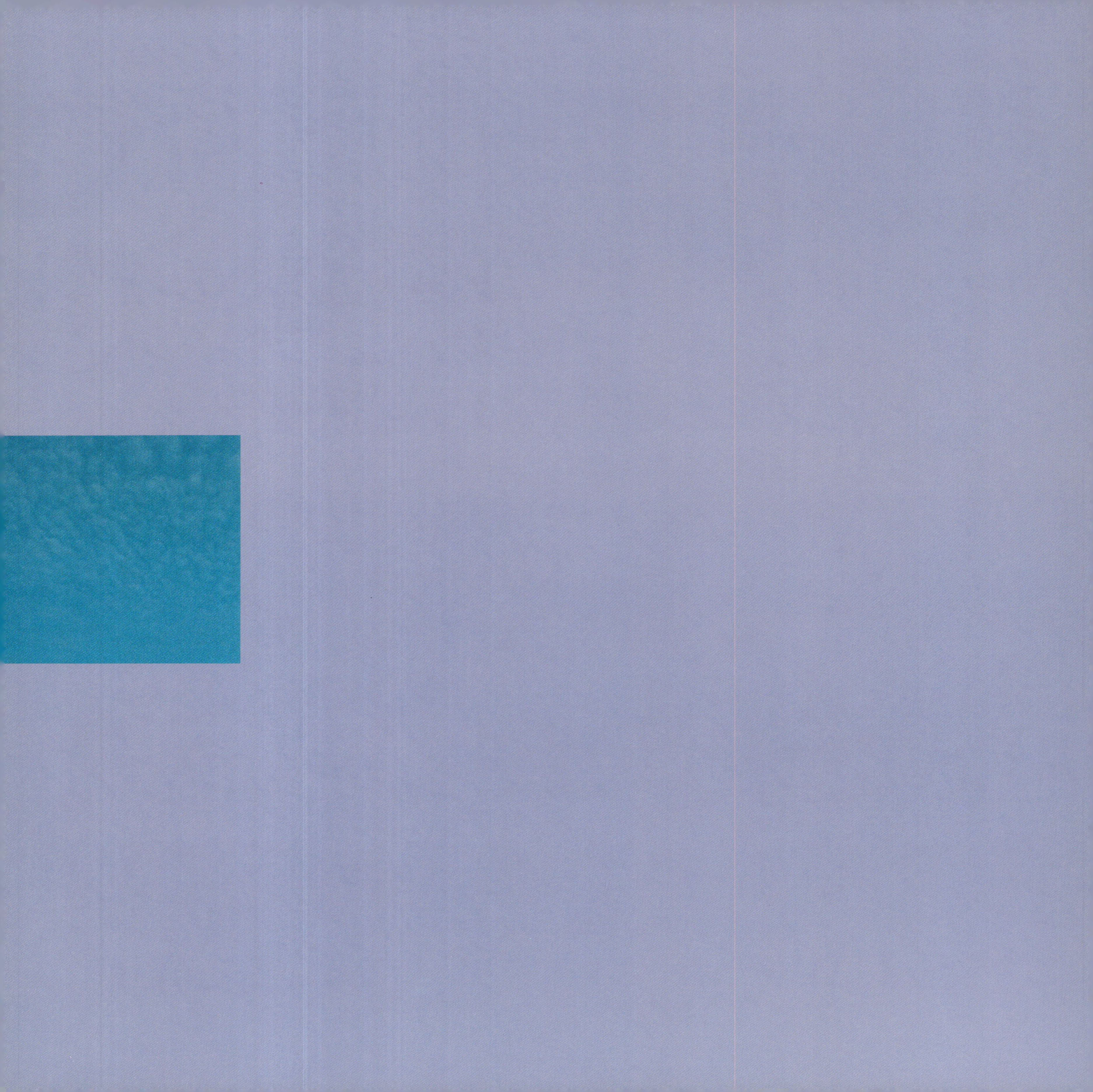

two PATTERN

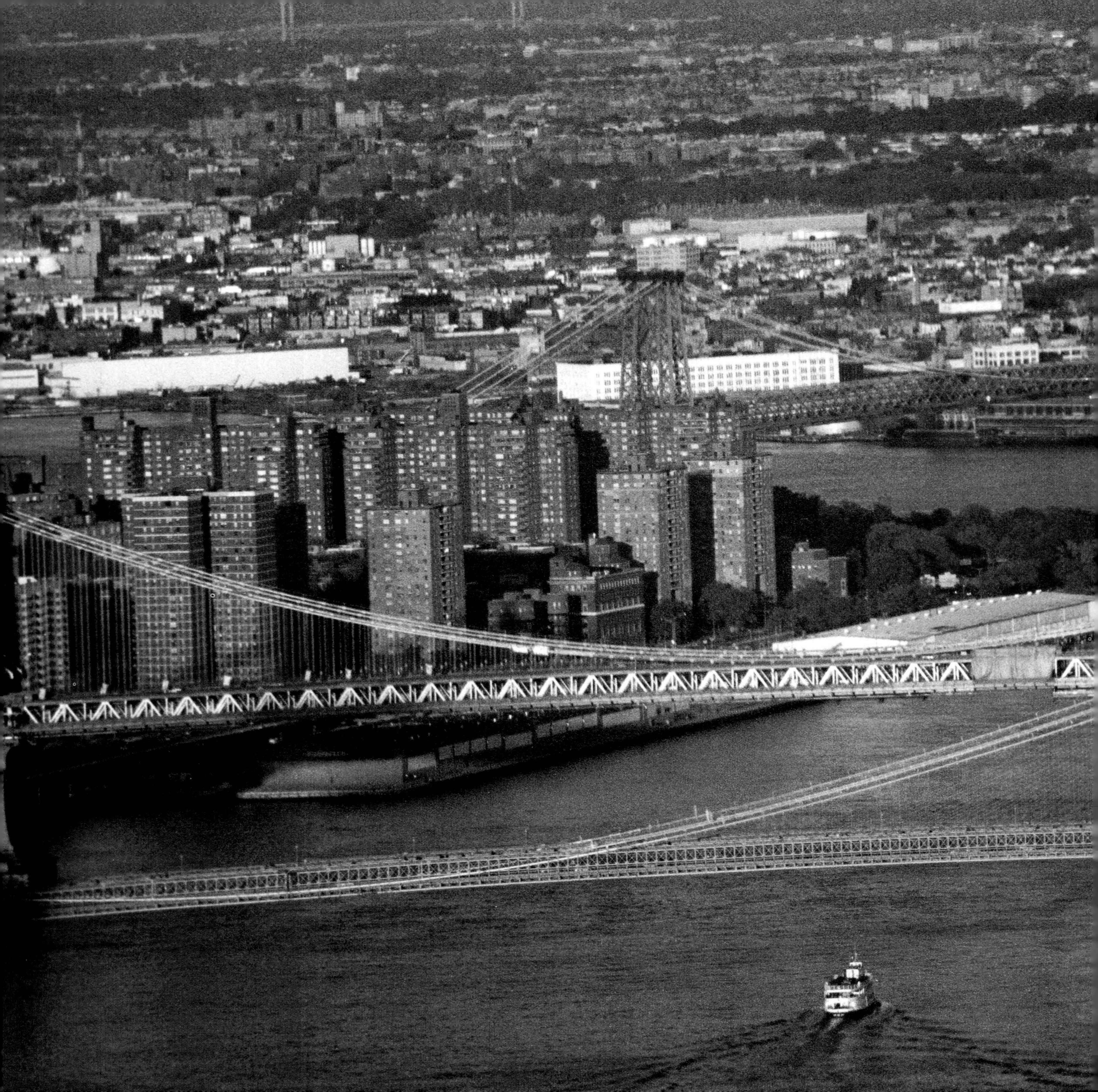

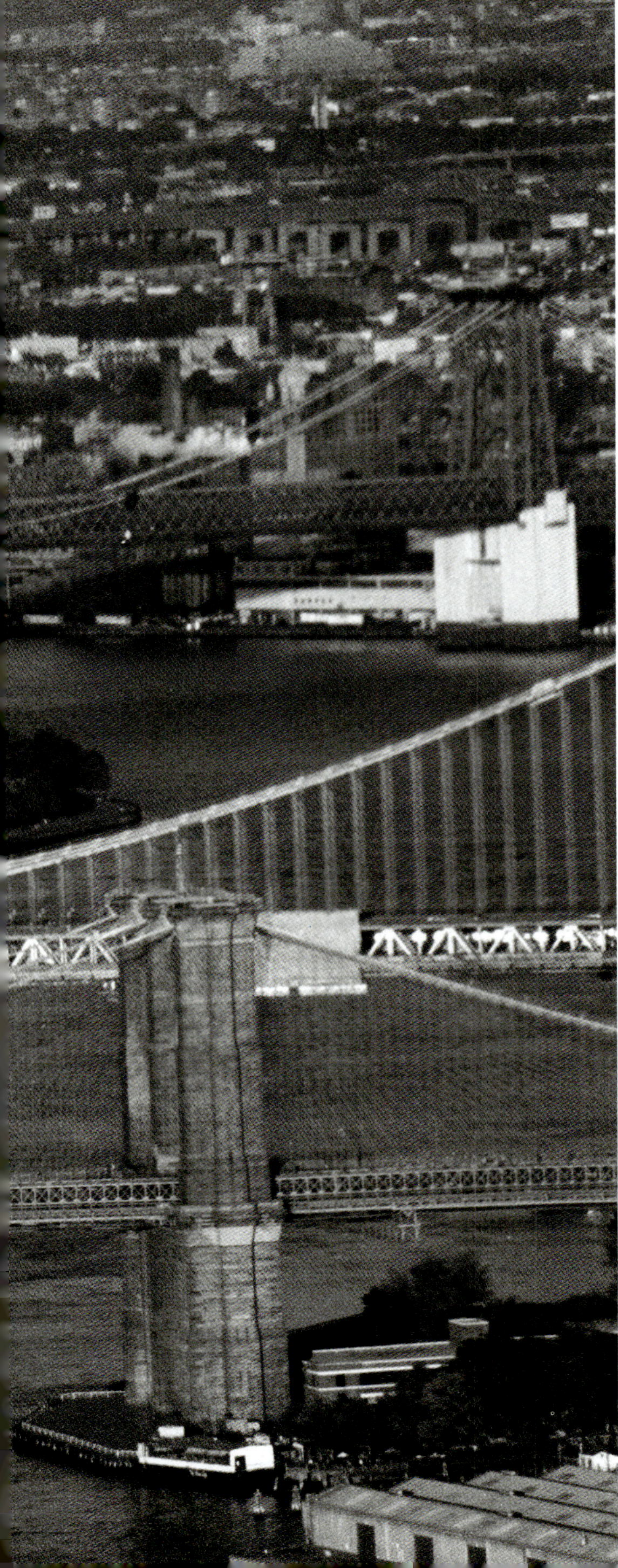

To one who has been long in city pent,
'Tis very sweet to look into the fair
And open face of heaven, ~ to breathe a prayer
Full in the smile of the blue firmament.

JOHN KEATS

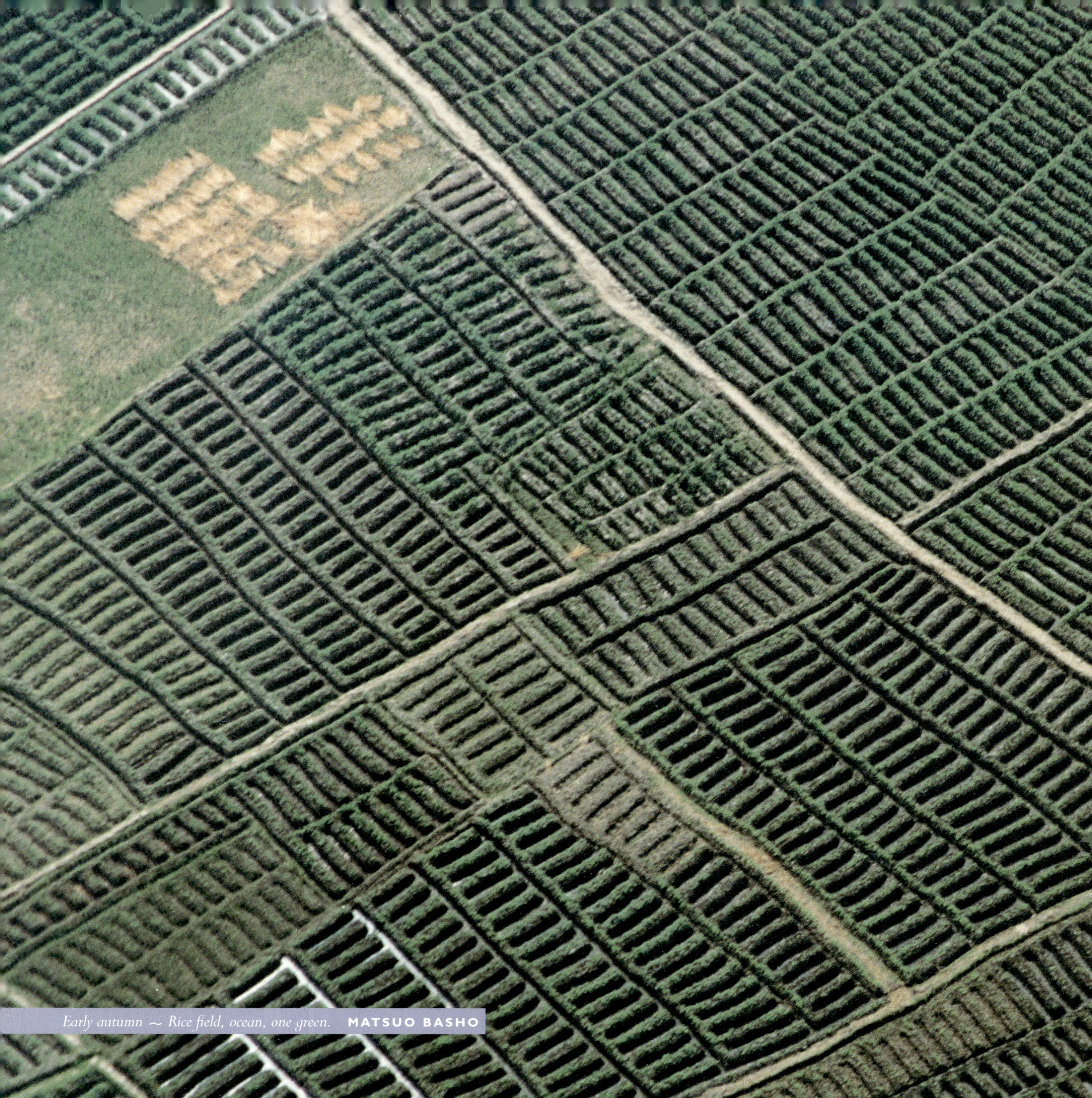

Early autumn ~ Rice field, ocean, one green. **MATSUO BASHO**

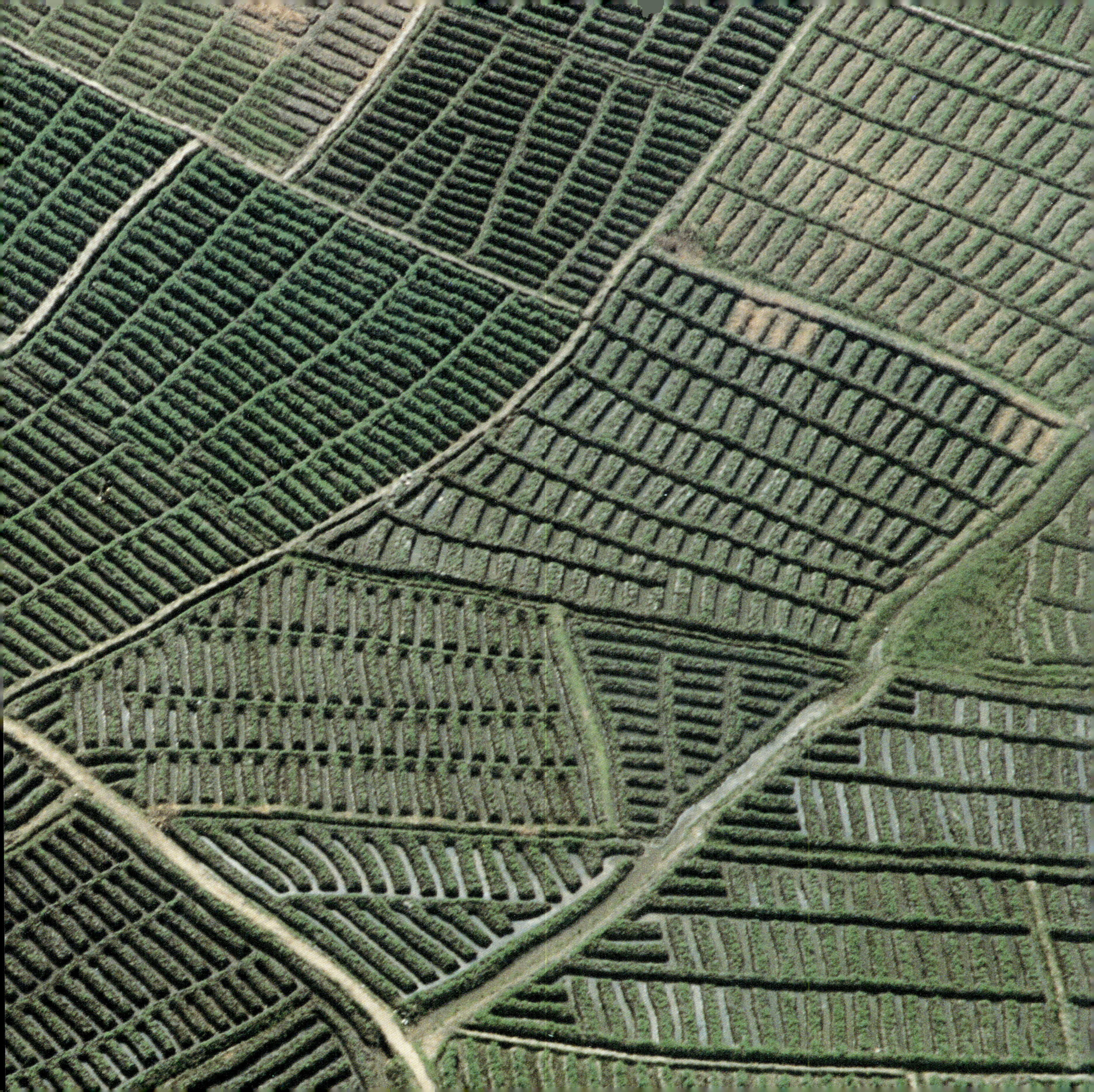

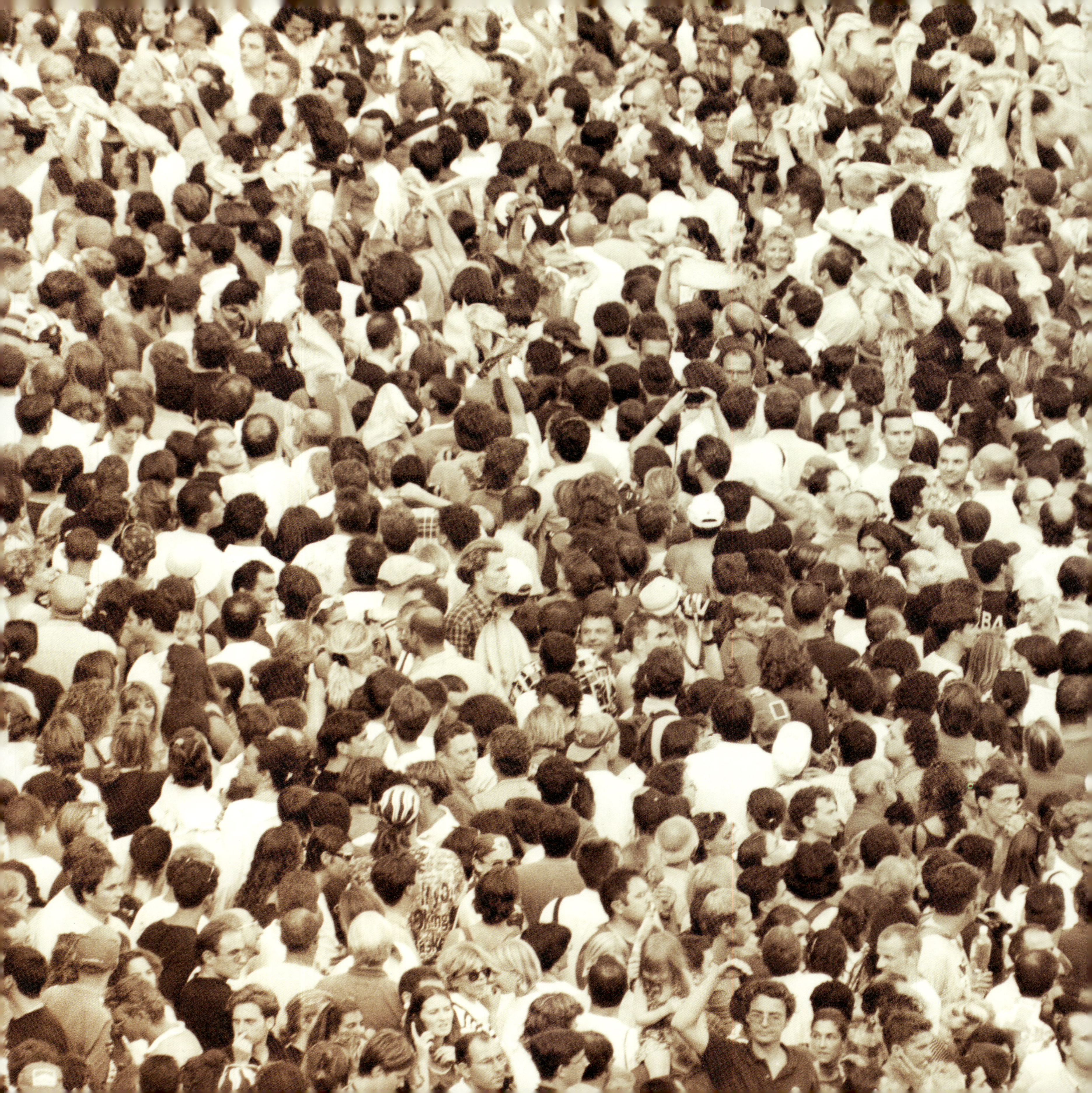

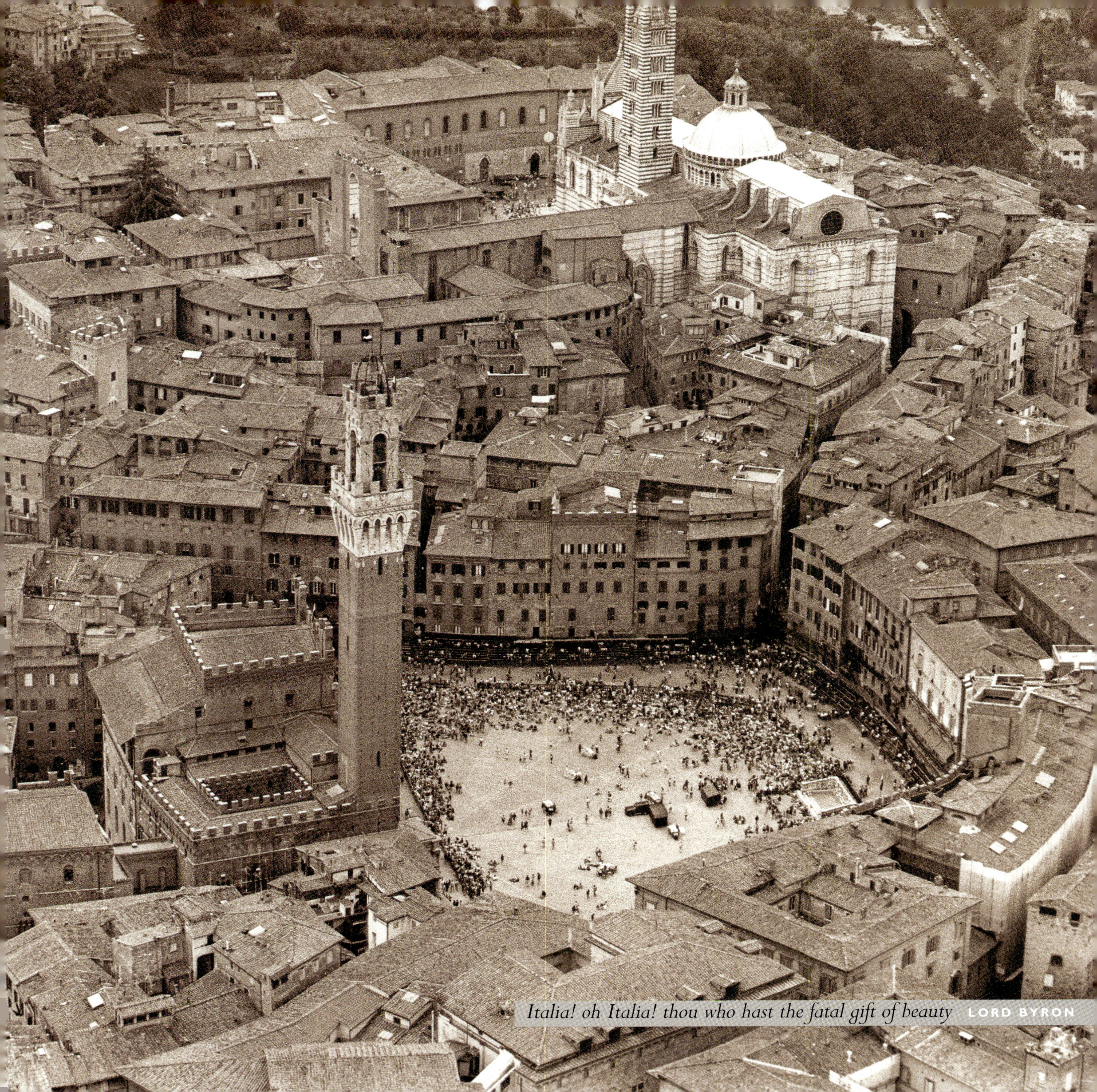

Italia! oh Italia! thou who hast the fatal gift of beauty LORD BYRON

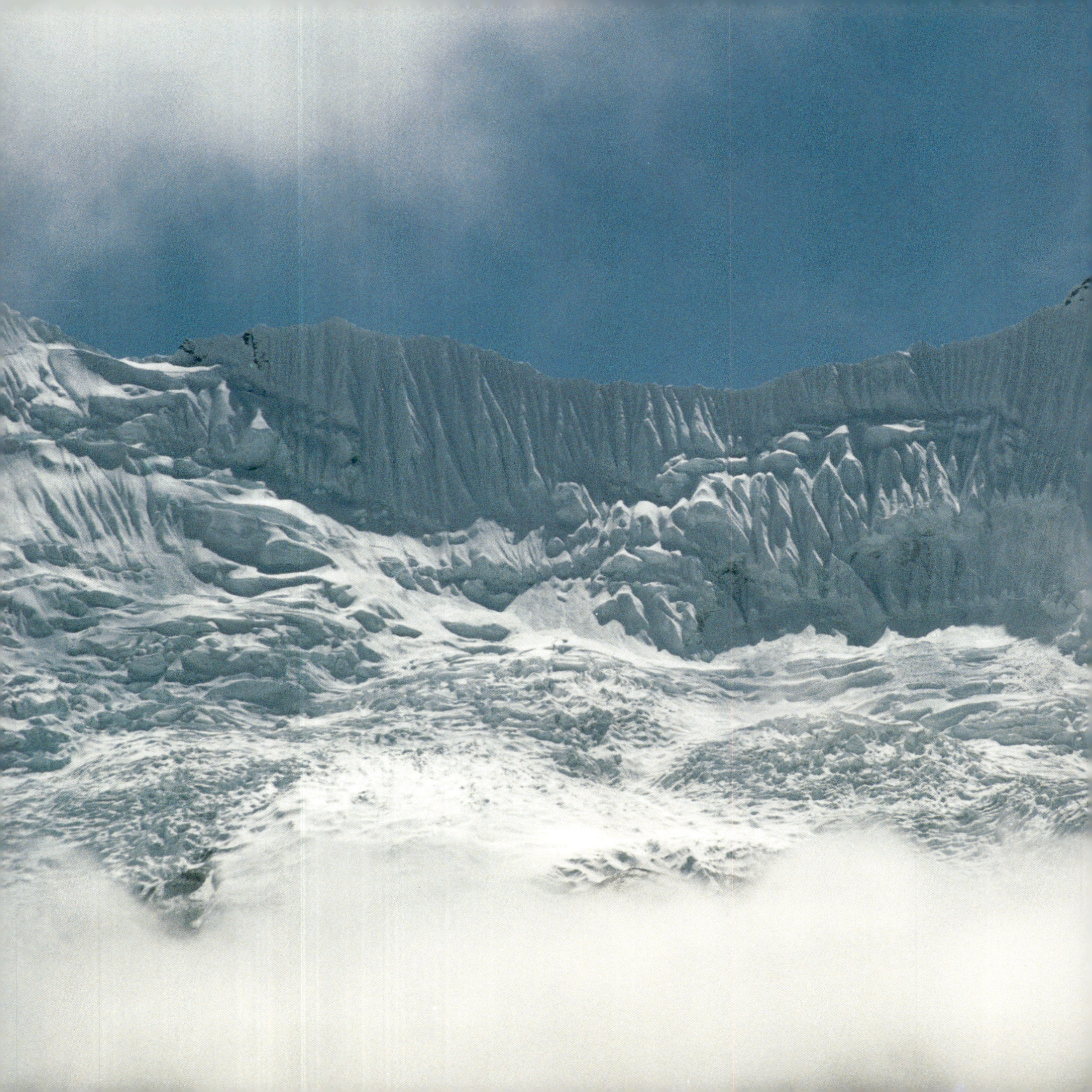

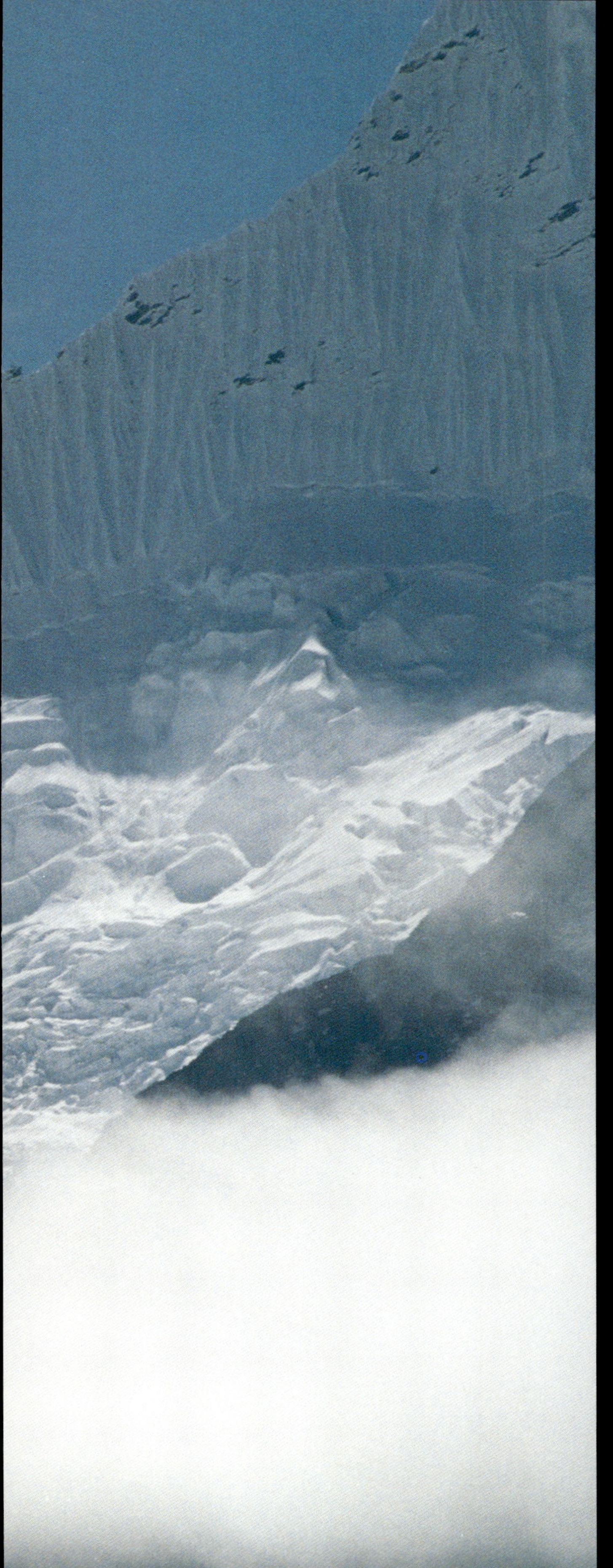

This is the closest to God
I am ever going to get alive.

PAUL SILLITOE,
WHILST CLIMBING THE
HIMALAYA WITH ME

Come away from the din.

Come away to the quiet fields,

over which the great sky stretches,

and where, between us and the stars,

there lies but silence;

and there, in the stillness

let us listen to the voice

that is speaking within us.

JEROME K. JEROME

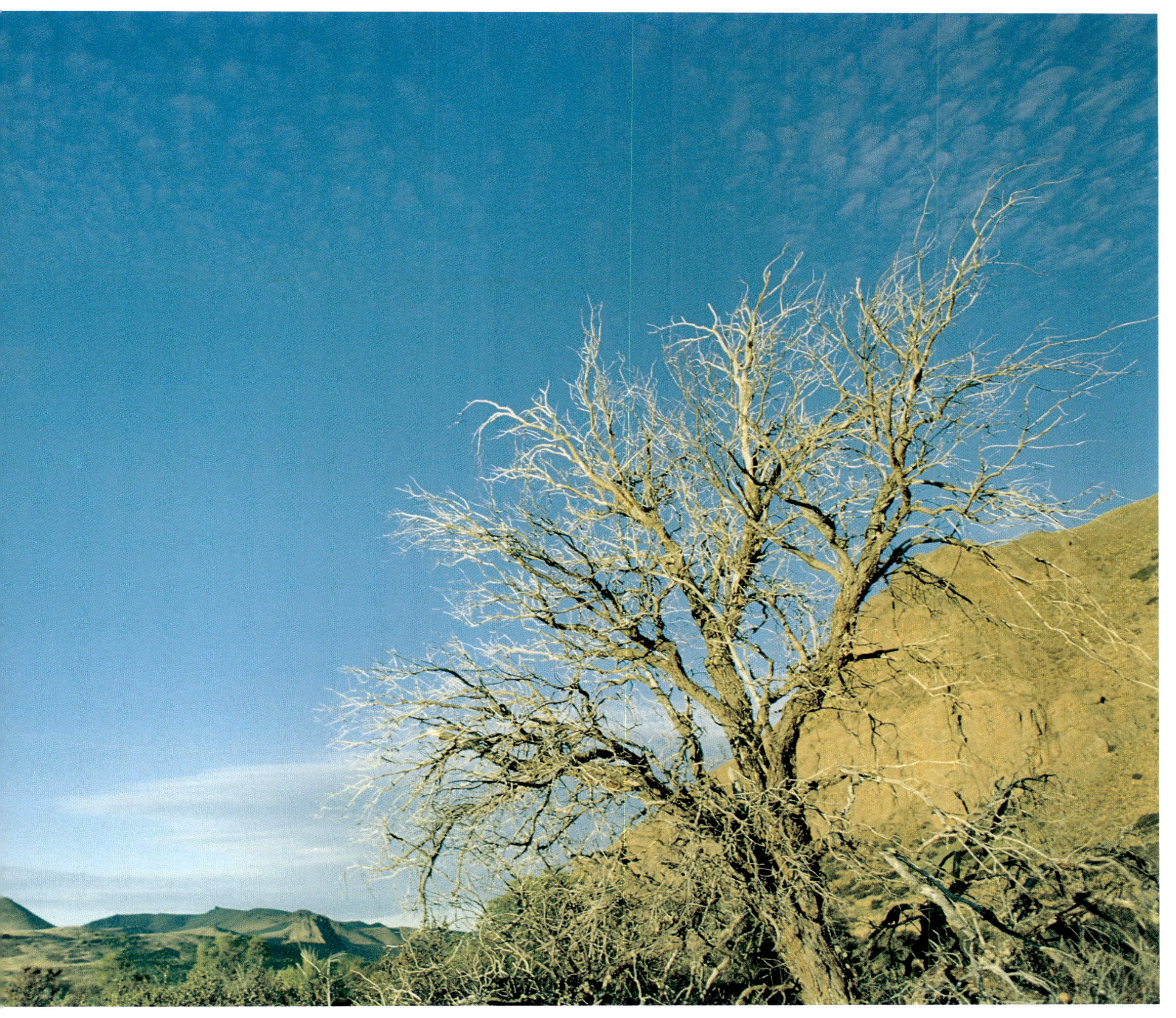

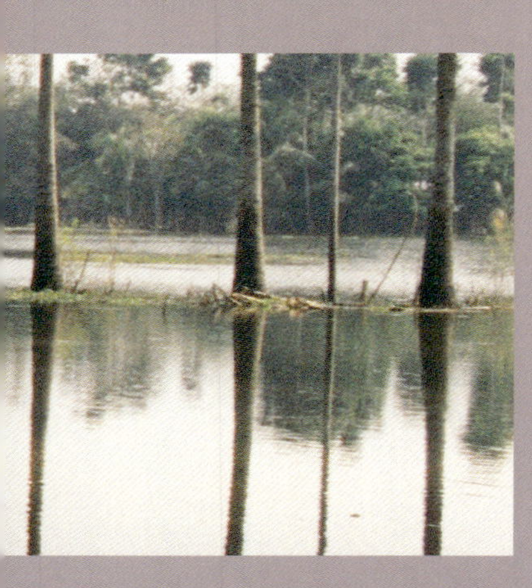

three REFLECTION

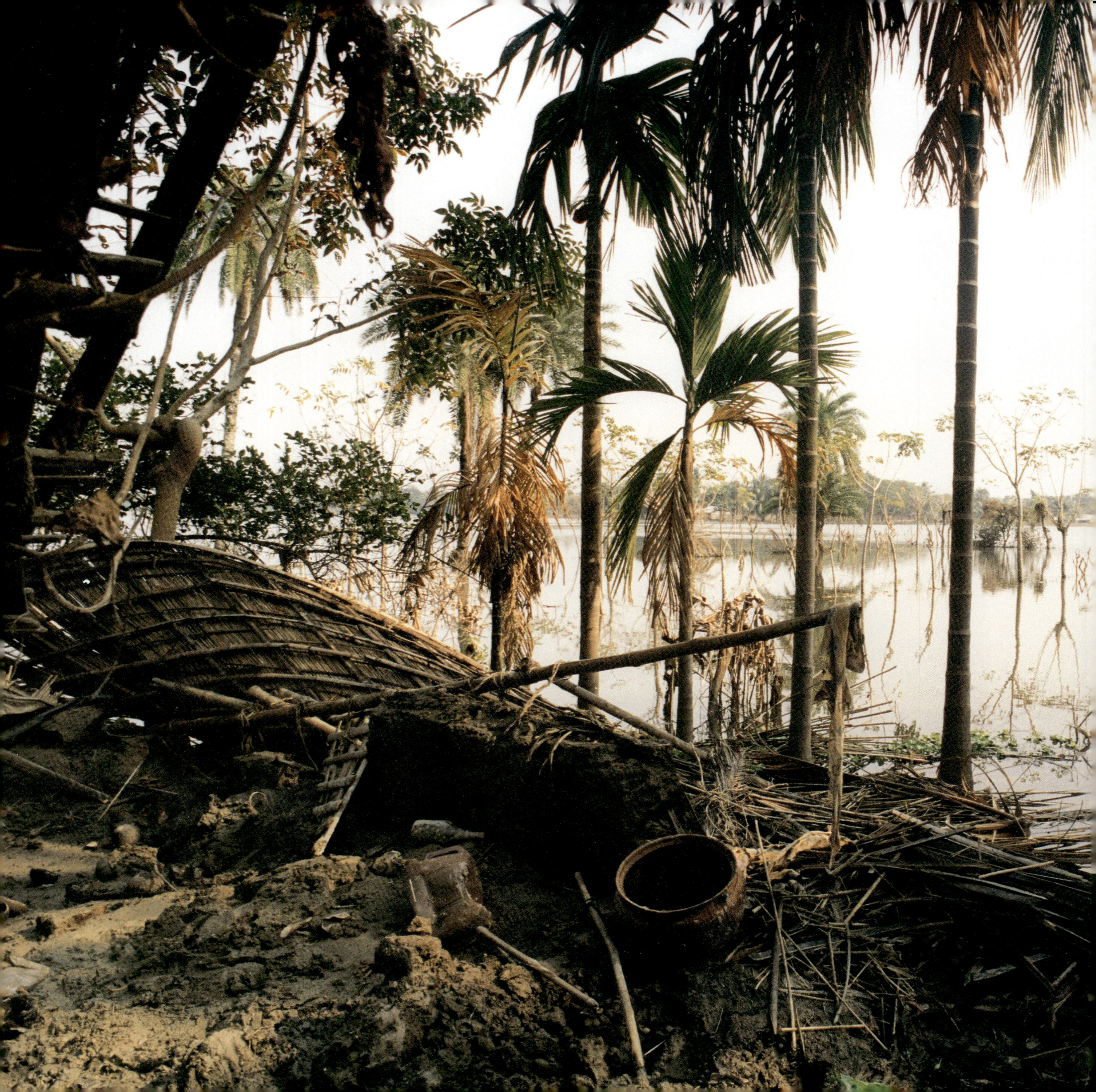

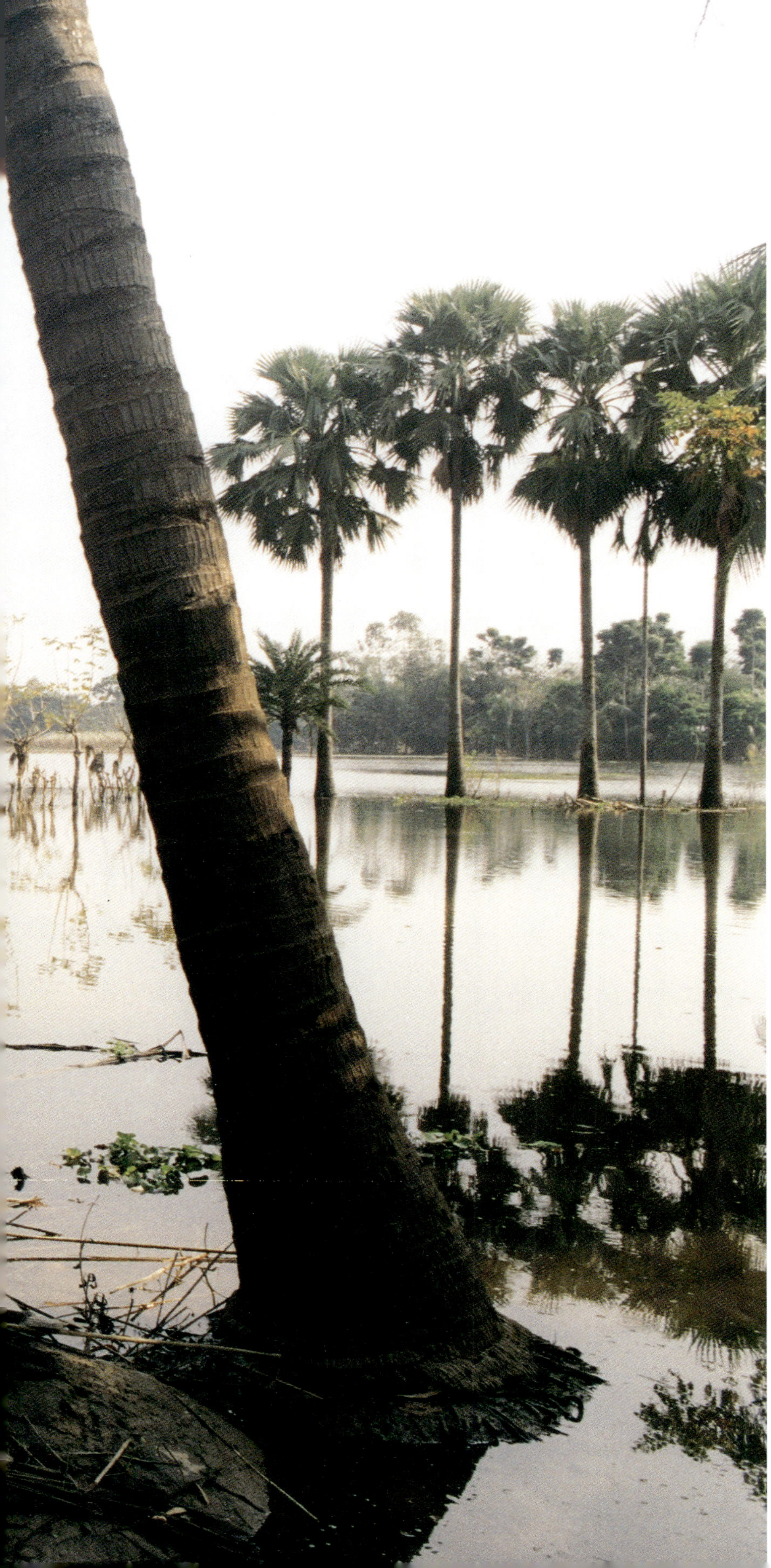

People are like stained-glass windows.
They sparkle and shine when the sun is out,
But when the darkness sets in, their true
Beauty is revealed only if there is a light from within.

ELISABETH KUBLER-ROSS

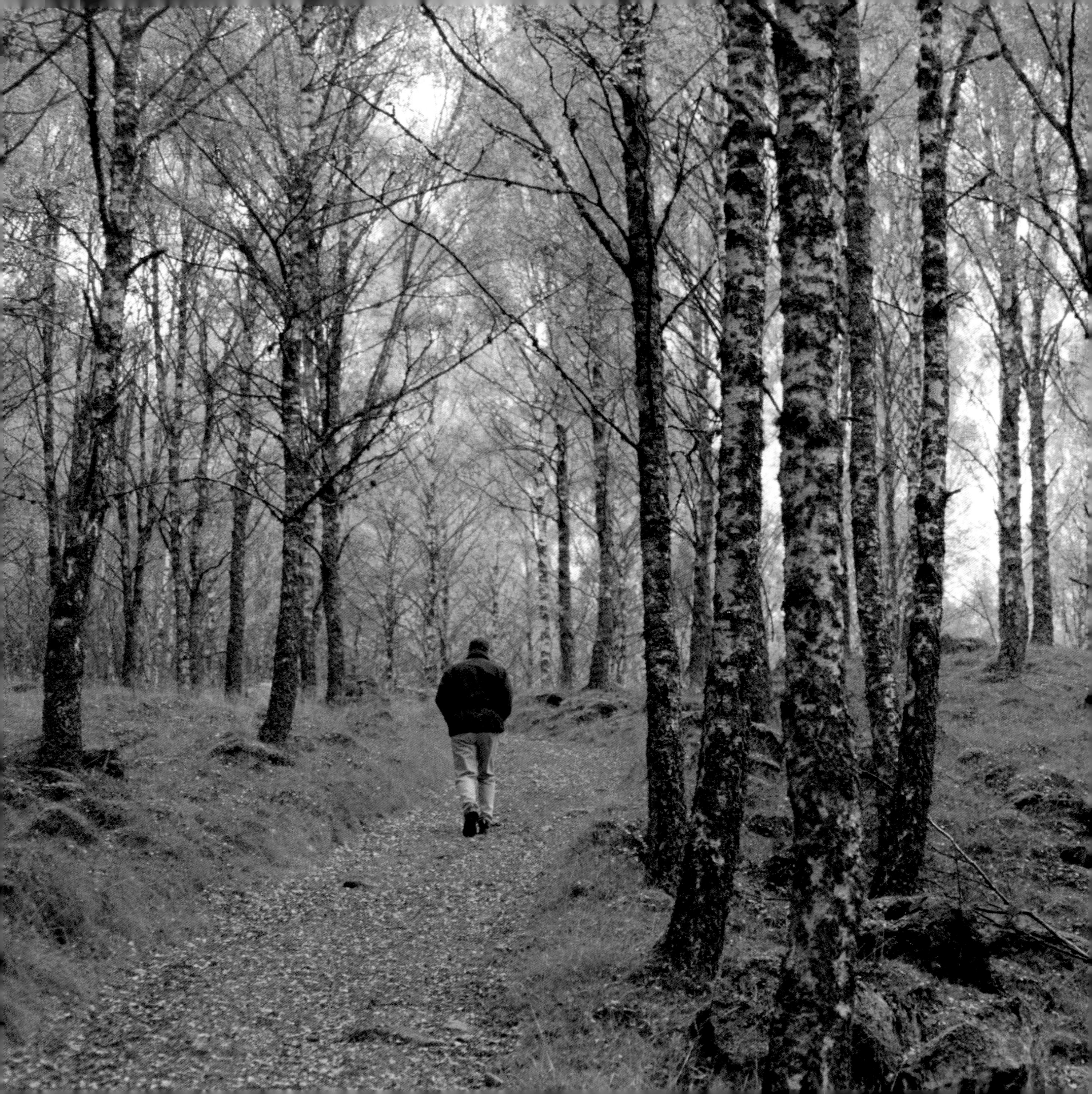

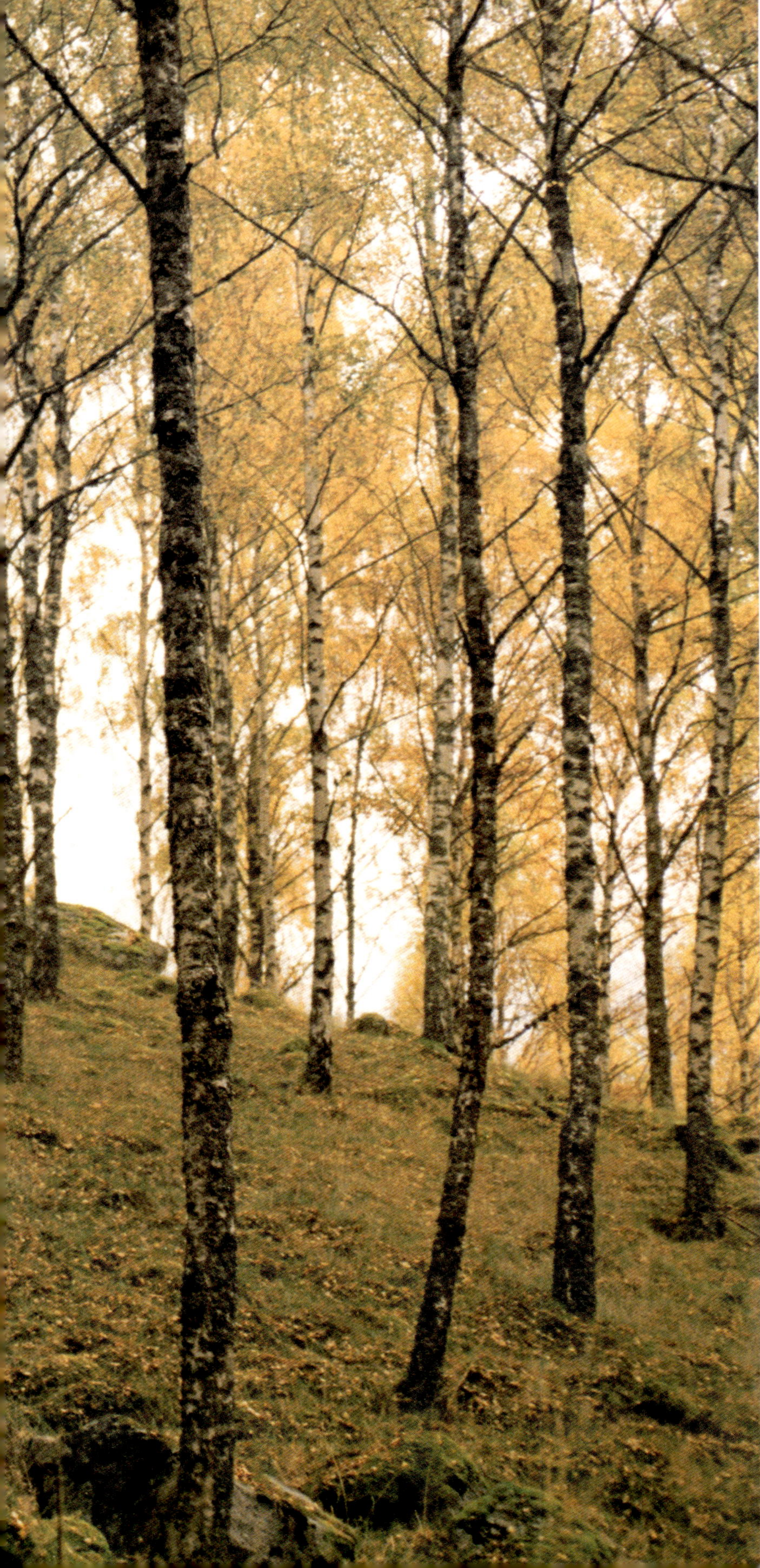

Loneliness is the poverty of self,
Solitude is the richness of self.

MAY SARTON

PEOPLE *travel to wonder at the height of* **MOUNTAINS**, *at the huge waves of the* **SEA**, *at the long courses of* **RIVERS**, *at the vast compass of the* **OCEAN**, *at the circular motion of the* **STARS**, *and they pass* **THEMSELVES** *by without wondering.*

ST AUGUSTINE

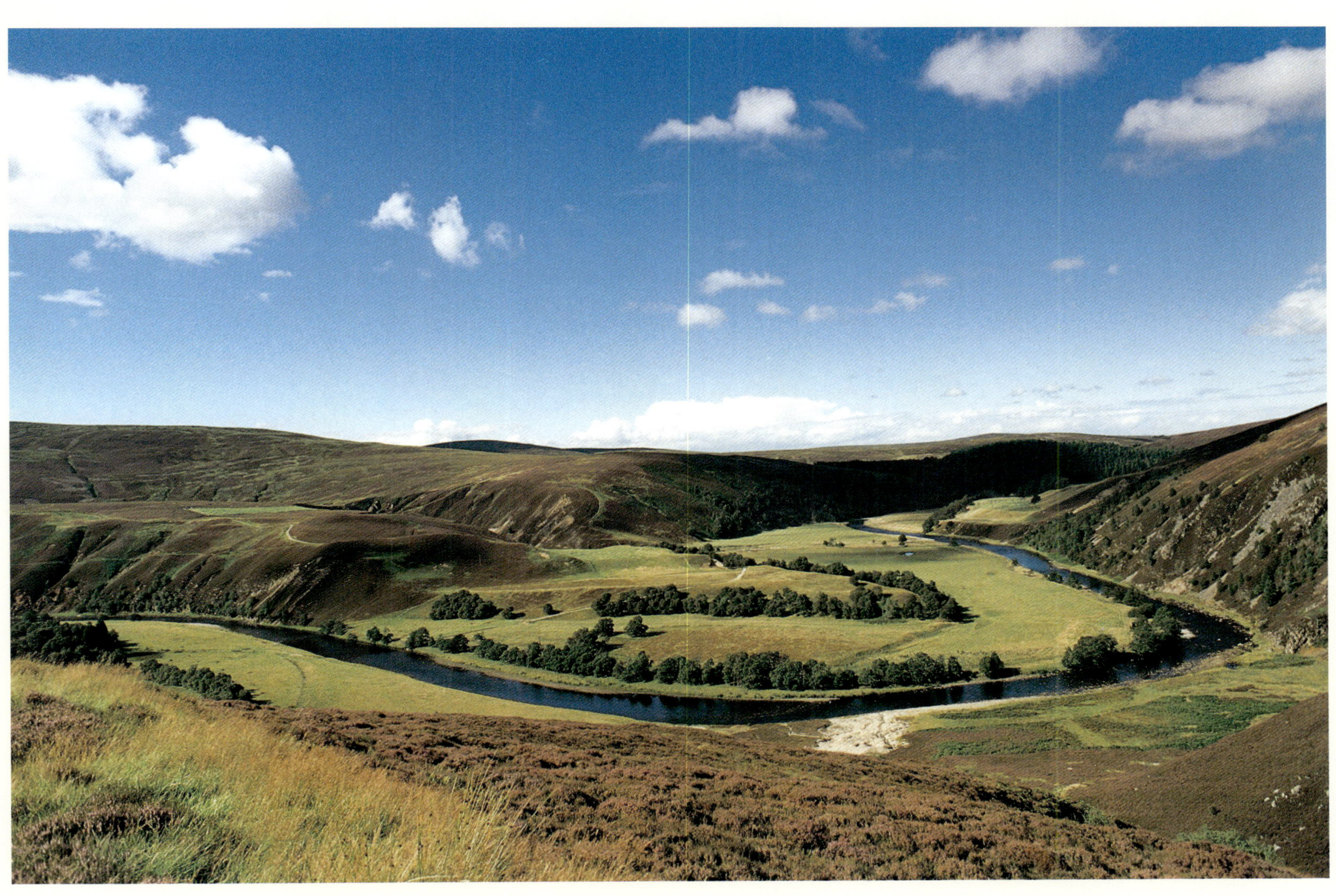

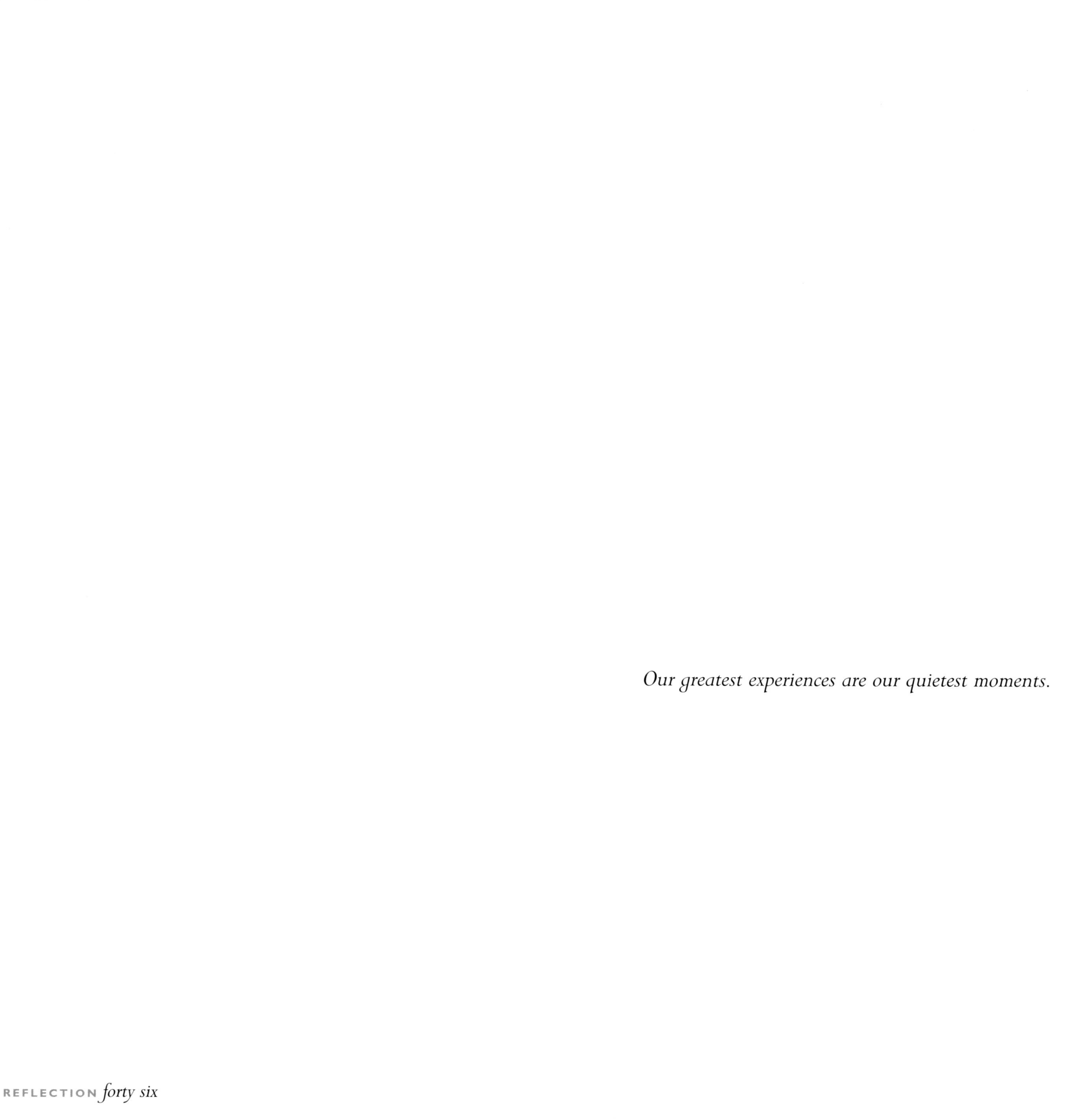

Our greatest experiences are our quietest moments.

FRIEDRICH NIETZSCHE

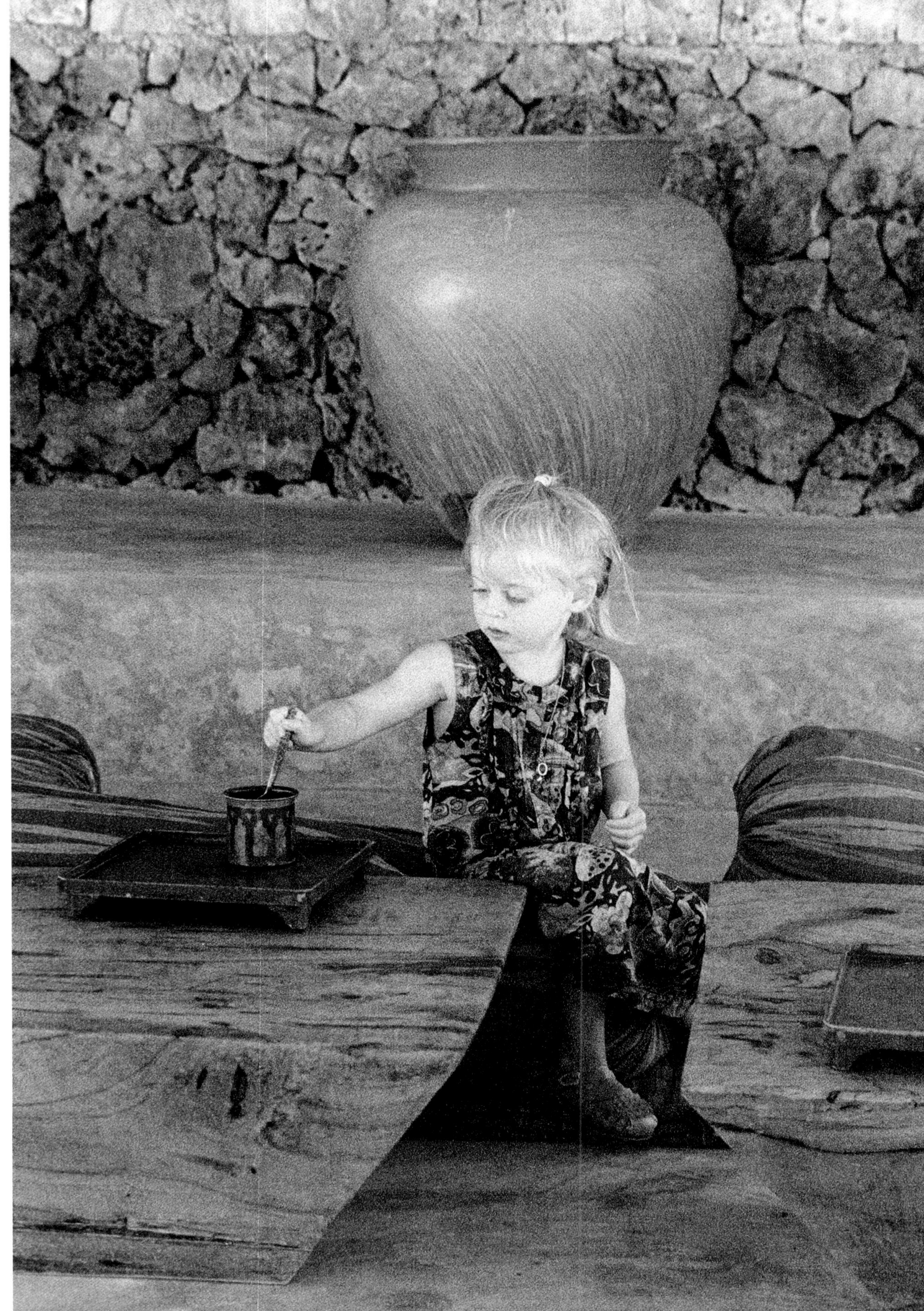

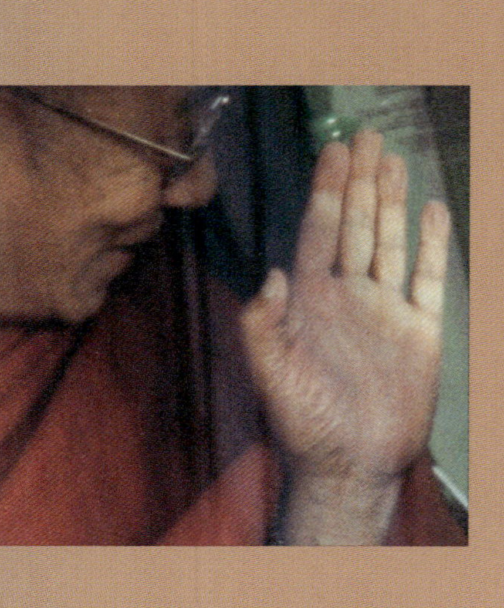

four CONTRAST

Our aspirations are our possibilities.

ROBERT BROWNING

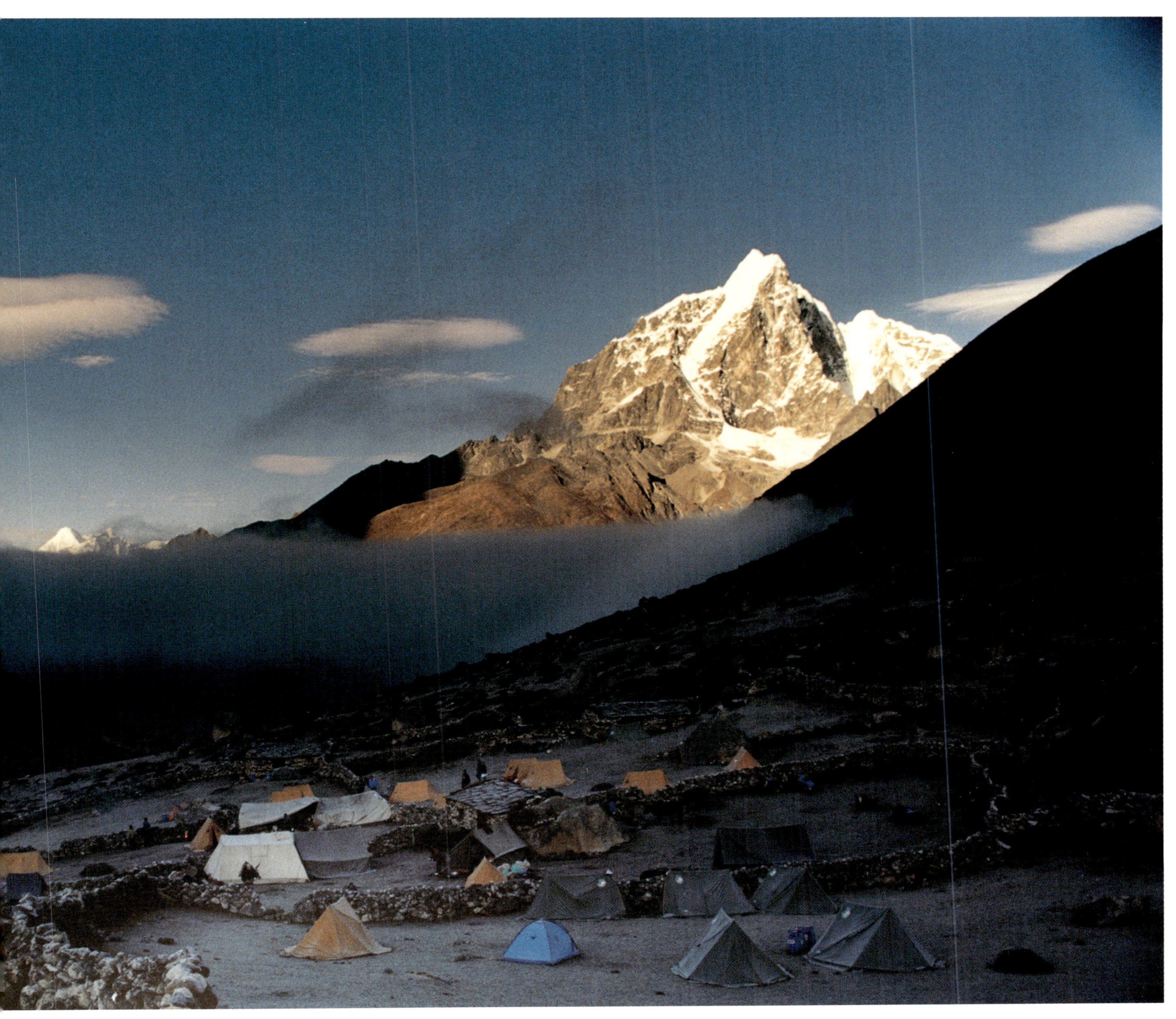

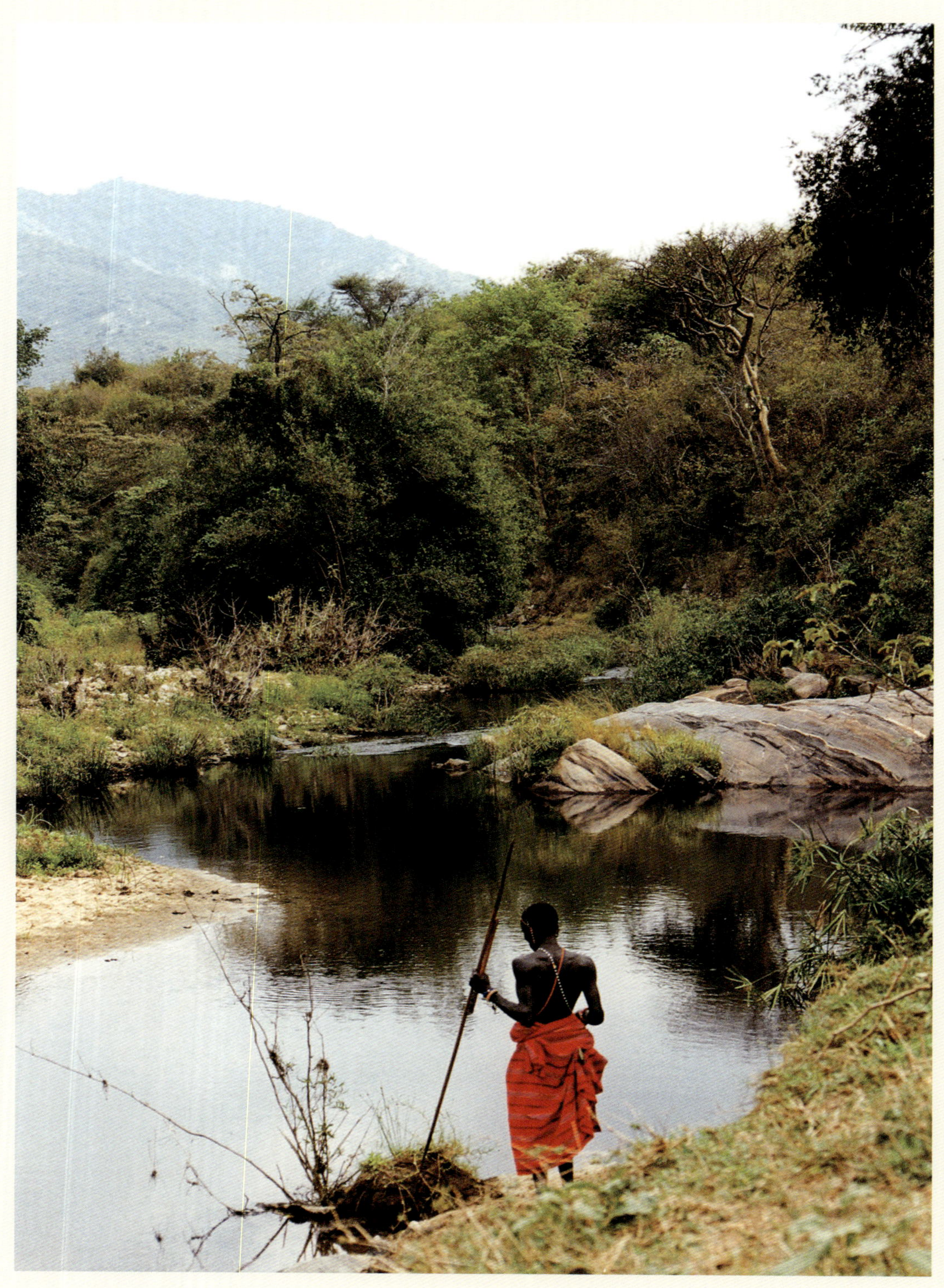

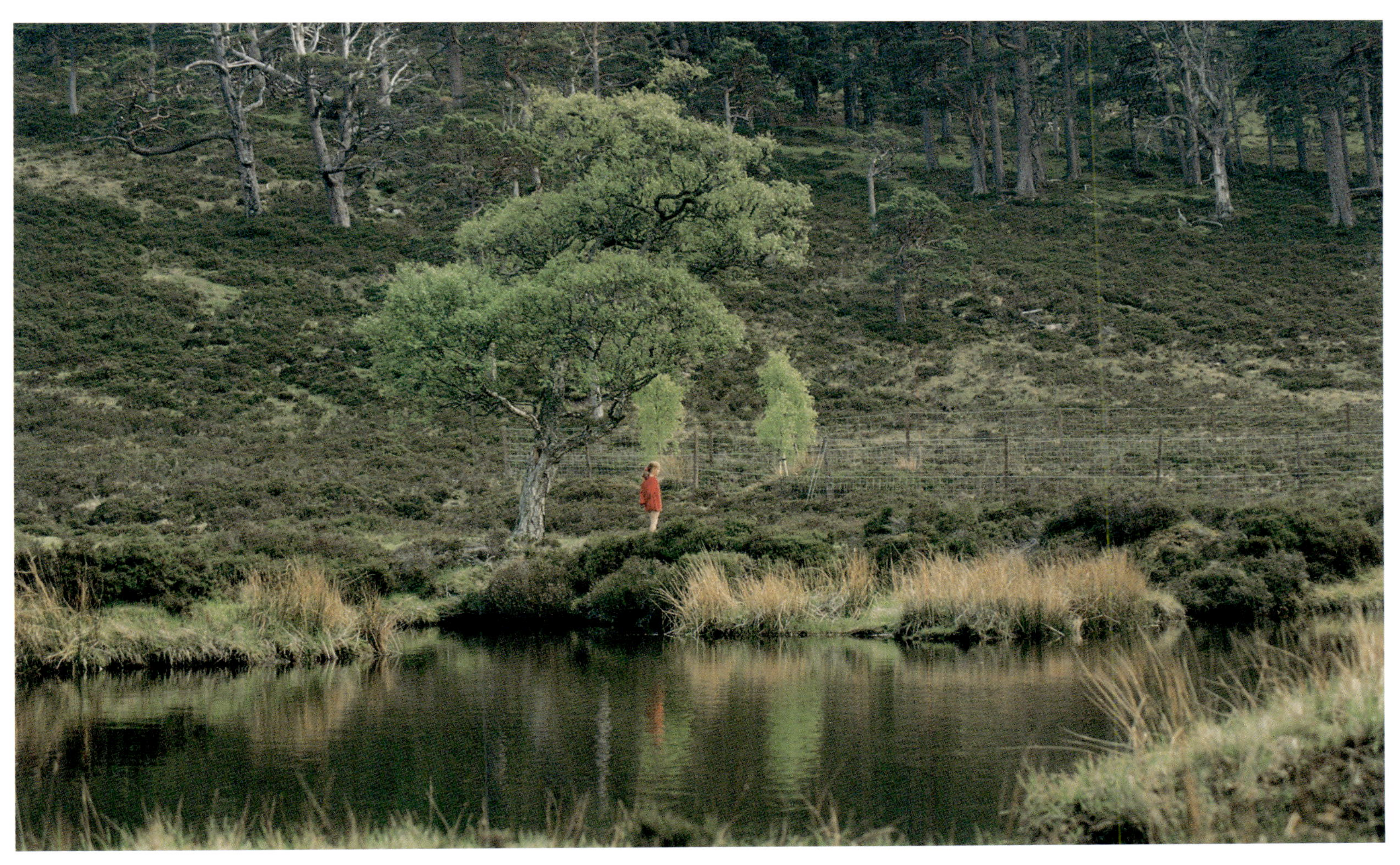

Friendship is a sheltering tree. SAMUEL TAYLOR COLERIDGE

NEVER

UNTIL

THEN

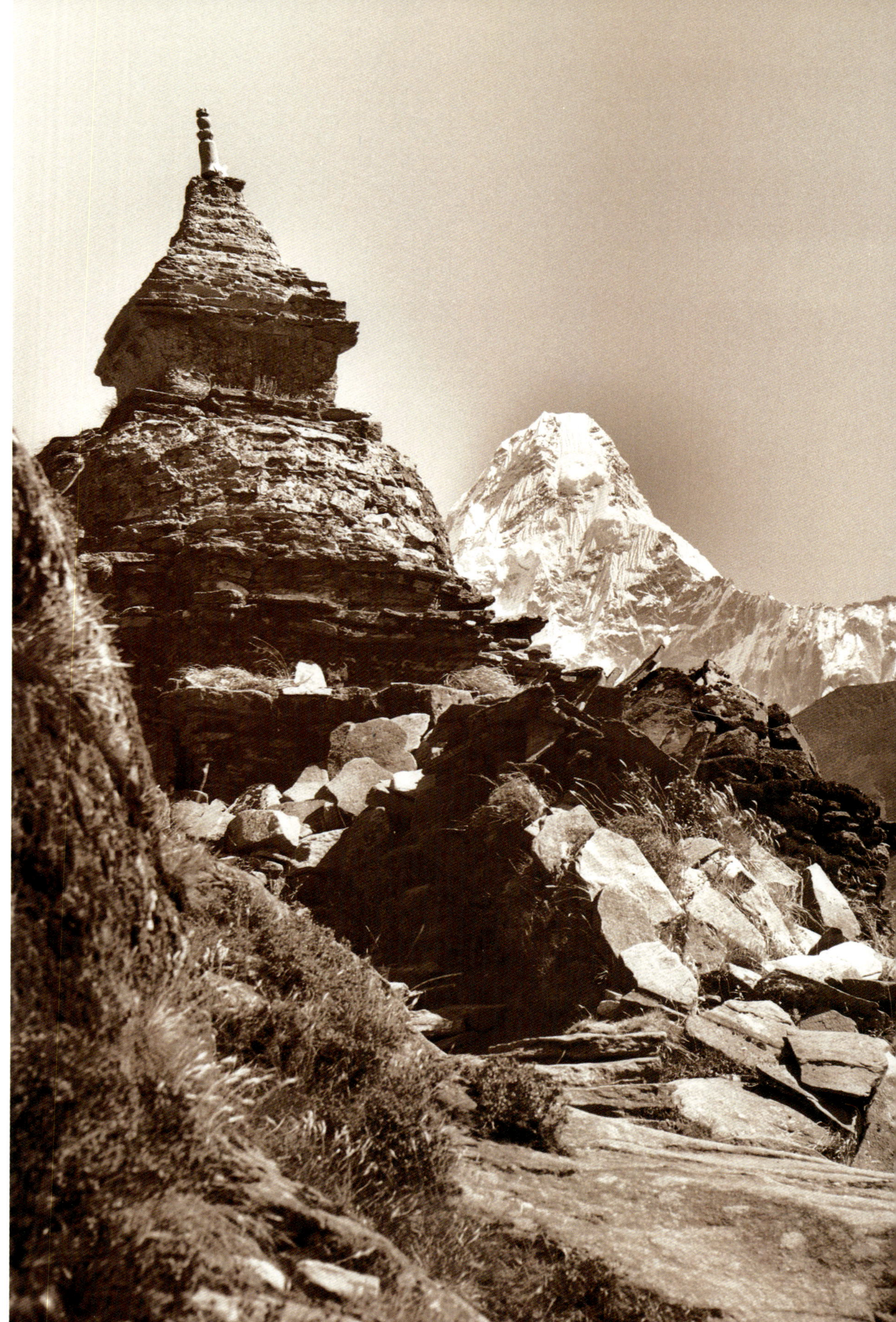

measure the height of a mountain,
you have reached the top,
you will see how low it was.

DAG HAMMARKSJOLD

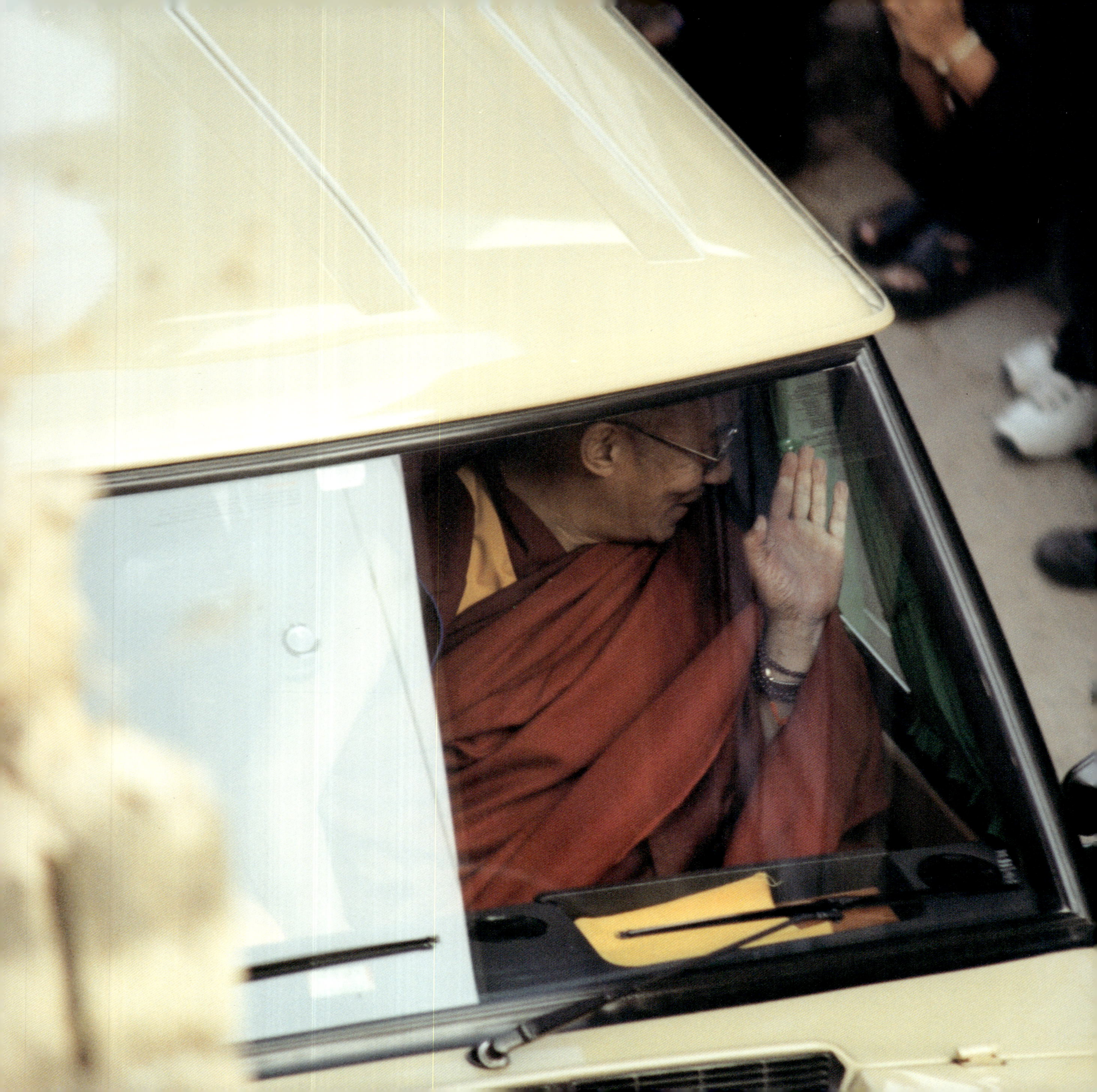

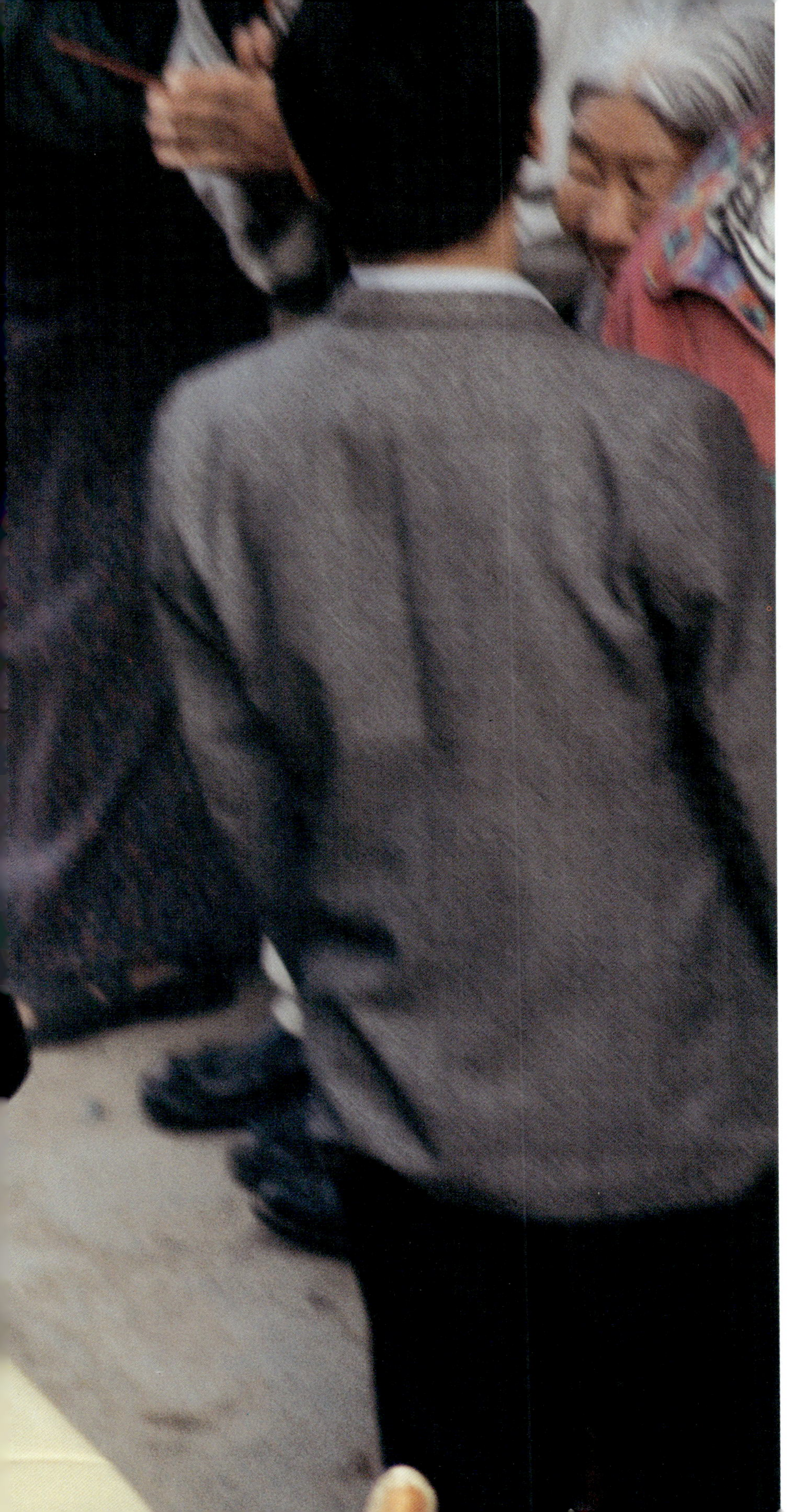

My religion is very simple.
My religion is kindness.

THE DALAI LAMA

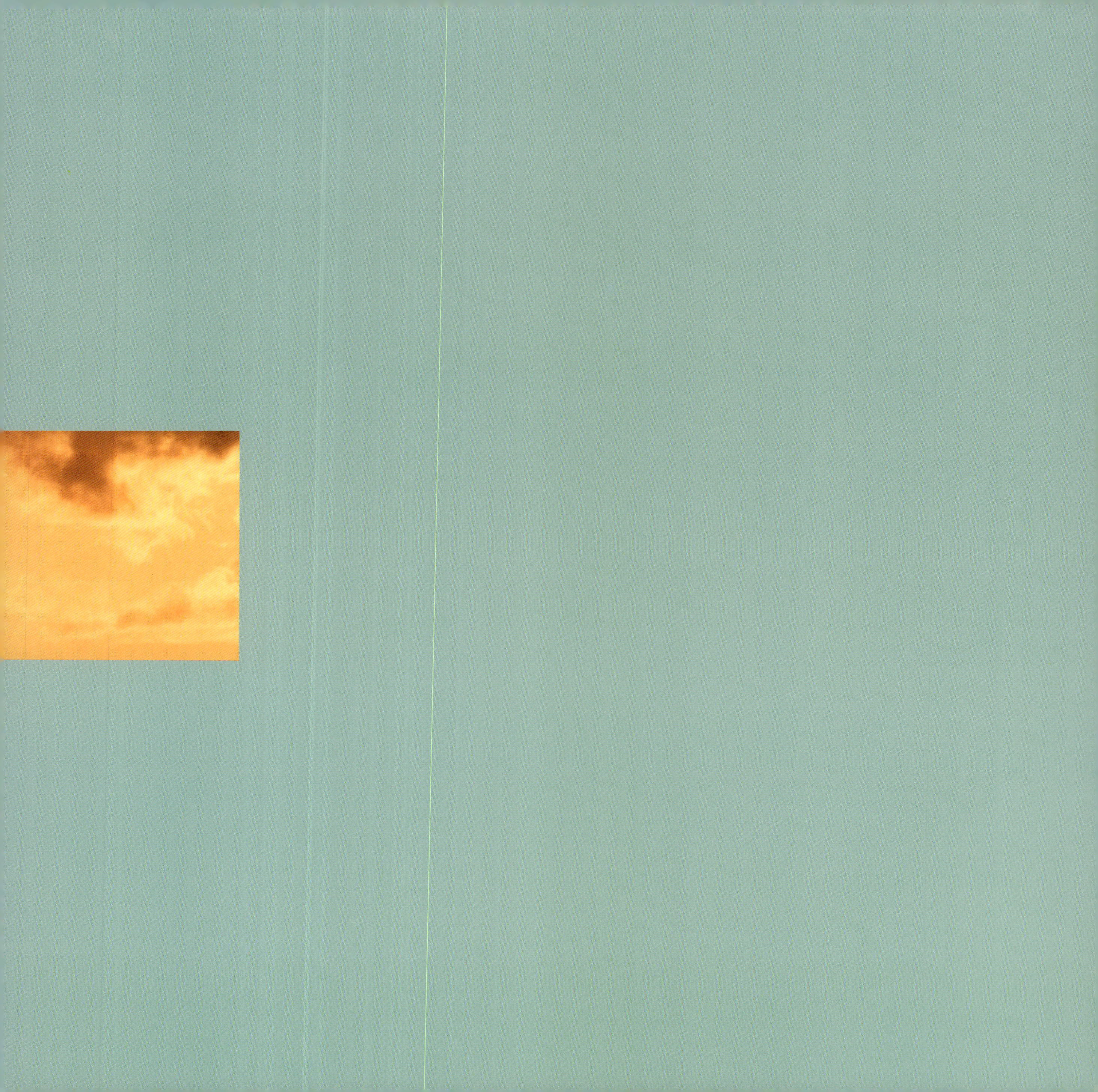

five LIGHT

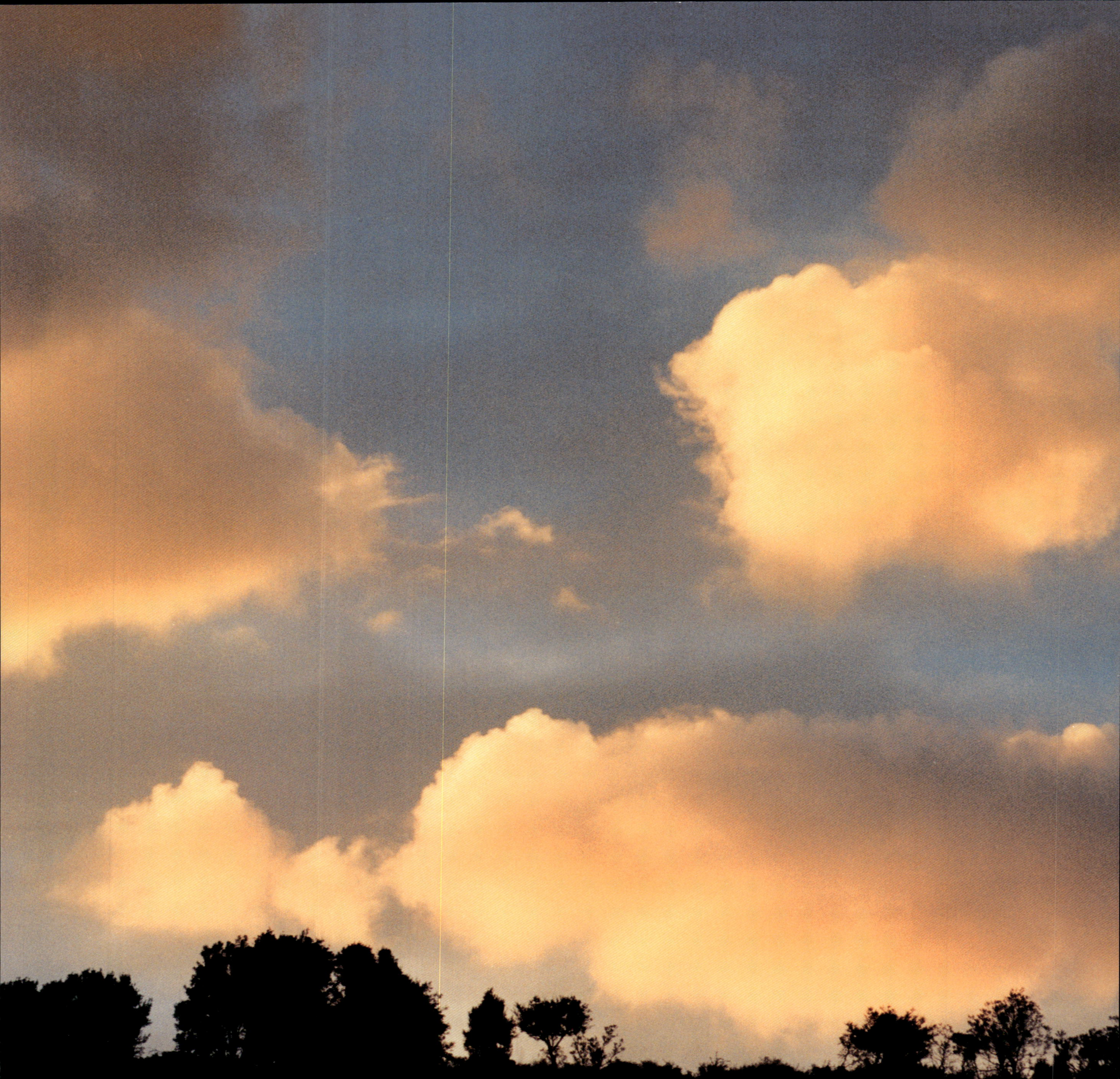

The ideals which have lighted my way, and time after time have given me new courage to face life cheerfully, have been kindness, beauty and truth.

ALBERT EINSTEIN

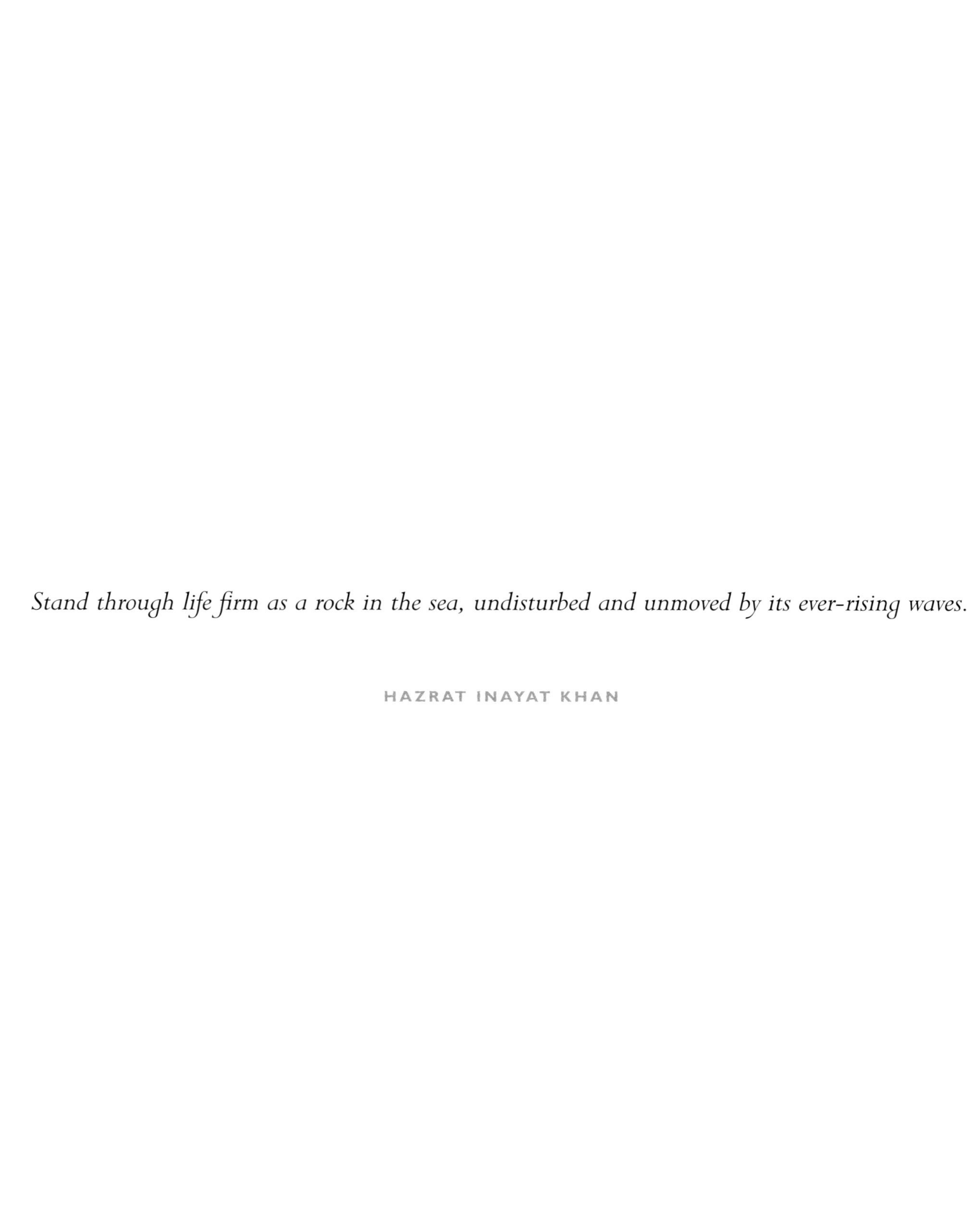

Stand through life firm as a rock in the sea, undisturbed and unmoved by its ever-rising waves.

HAZRAT INAYAT KHAN

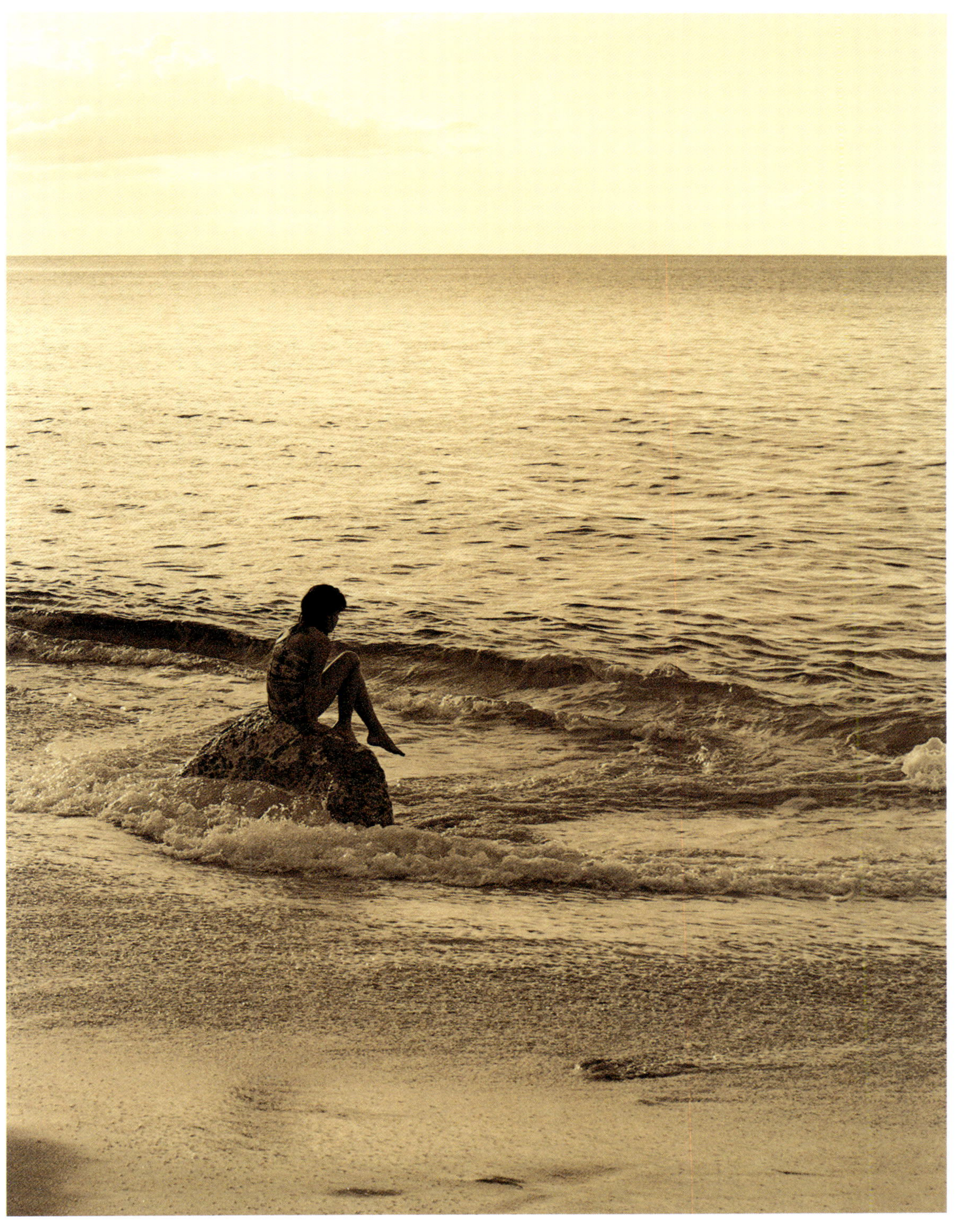

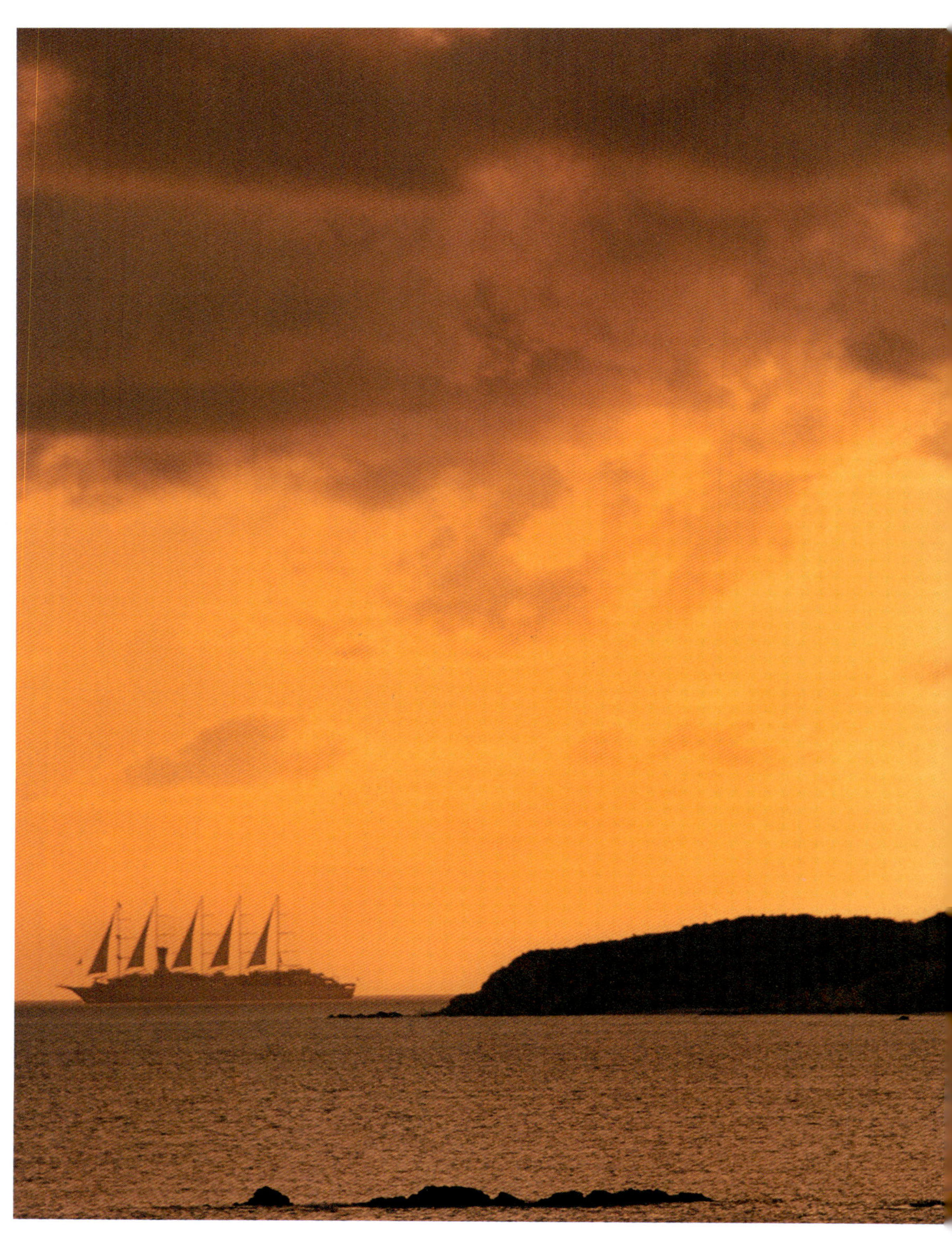

The winds of grace blow all the time.

All we need to do is set our sails. RAMAKRISHNA

Had I the heavens' embroidered cloths,
Enwrought with golden and silver light,
The blue and the dim and the dark cloths
Of night and light and the half-light,
I would spread the cloths under your feet:
But I, being poor, have only my dreams
I have spread my dreams under your feet;
Tread softly because you tread on my **DREAMS**

W. B. YEATS

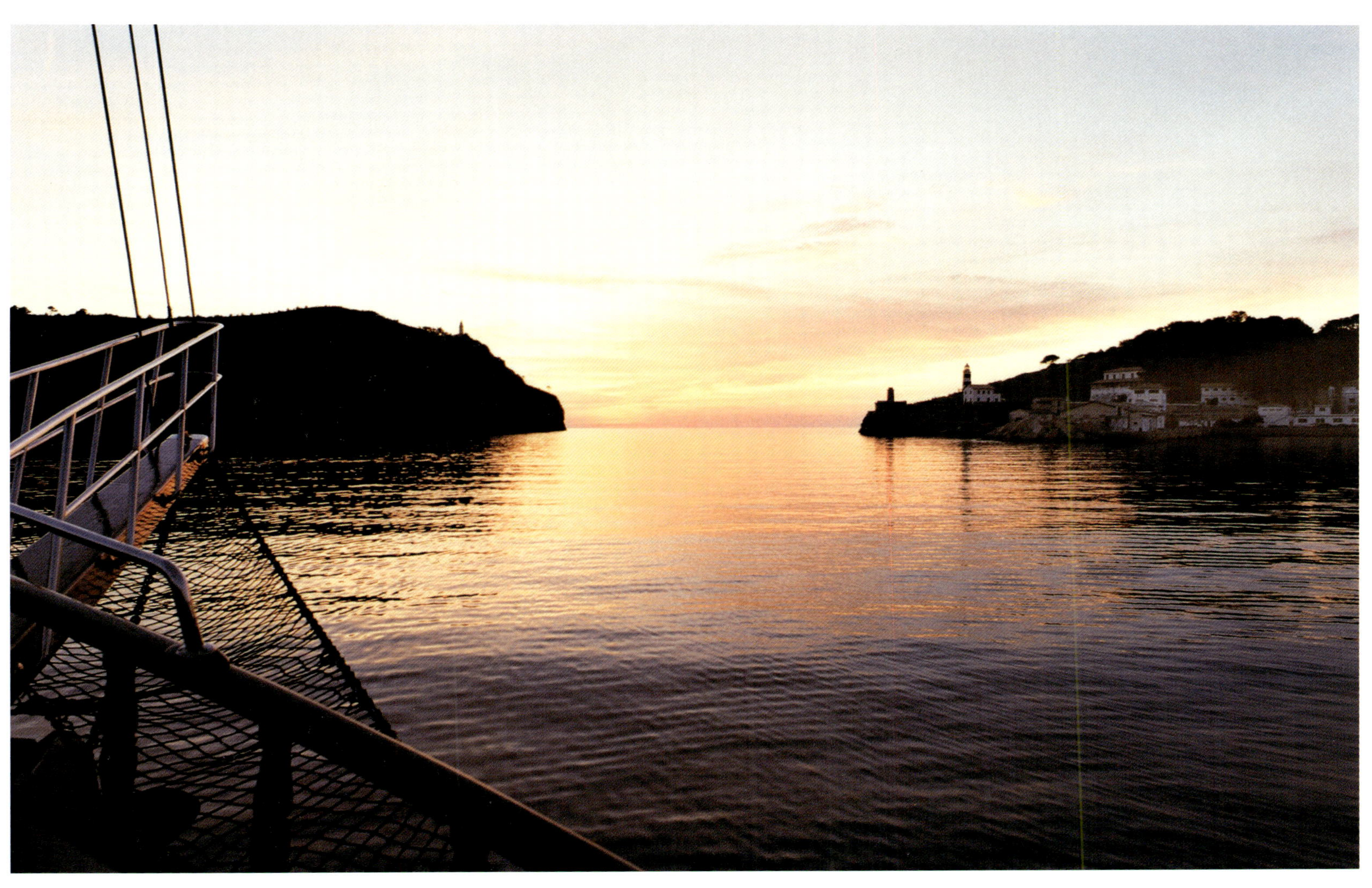

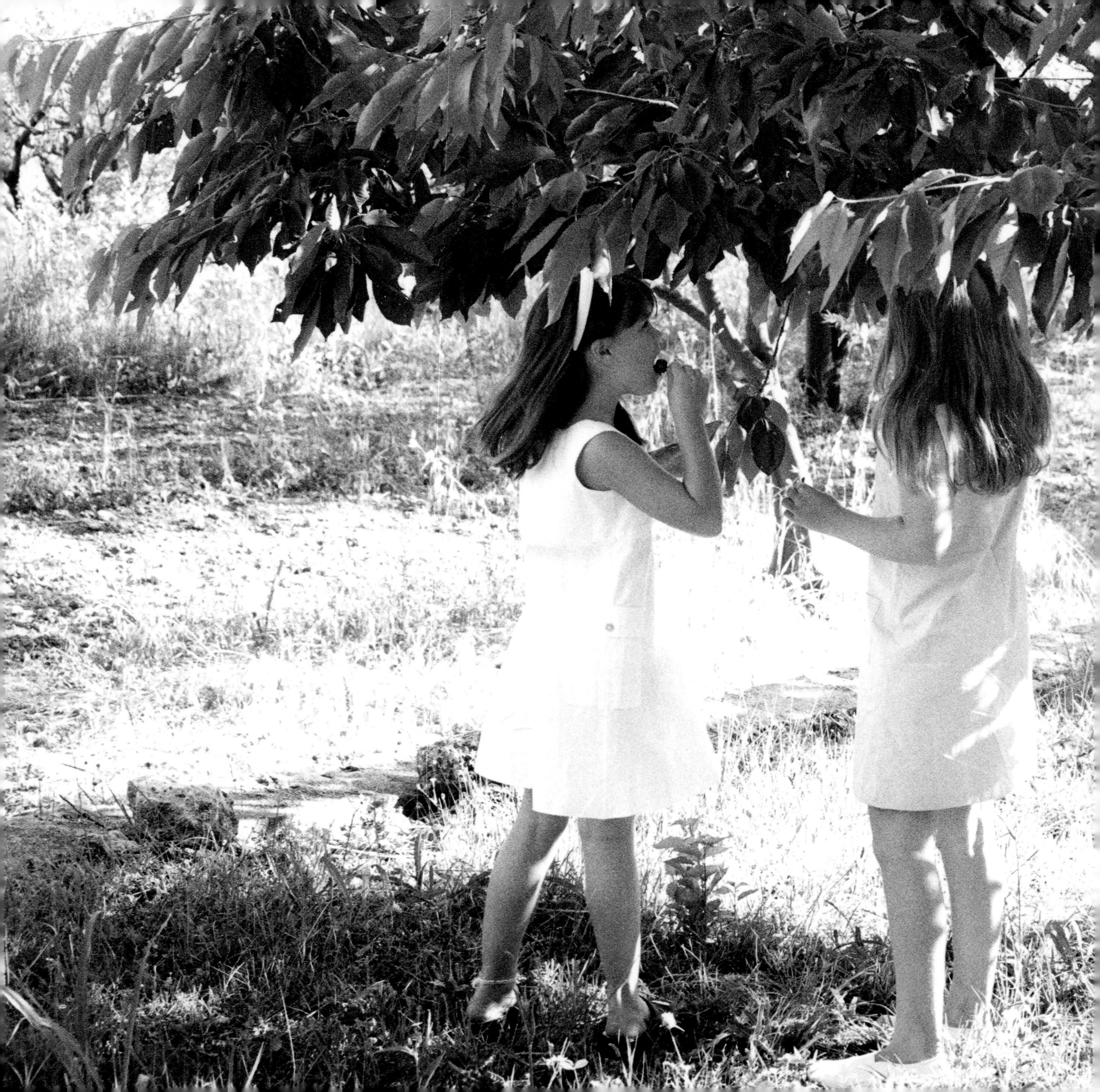

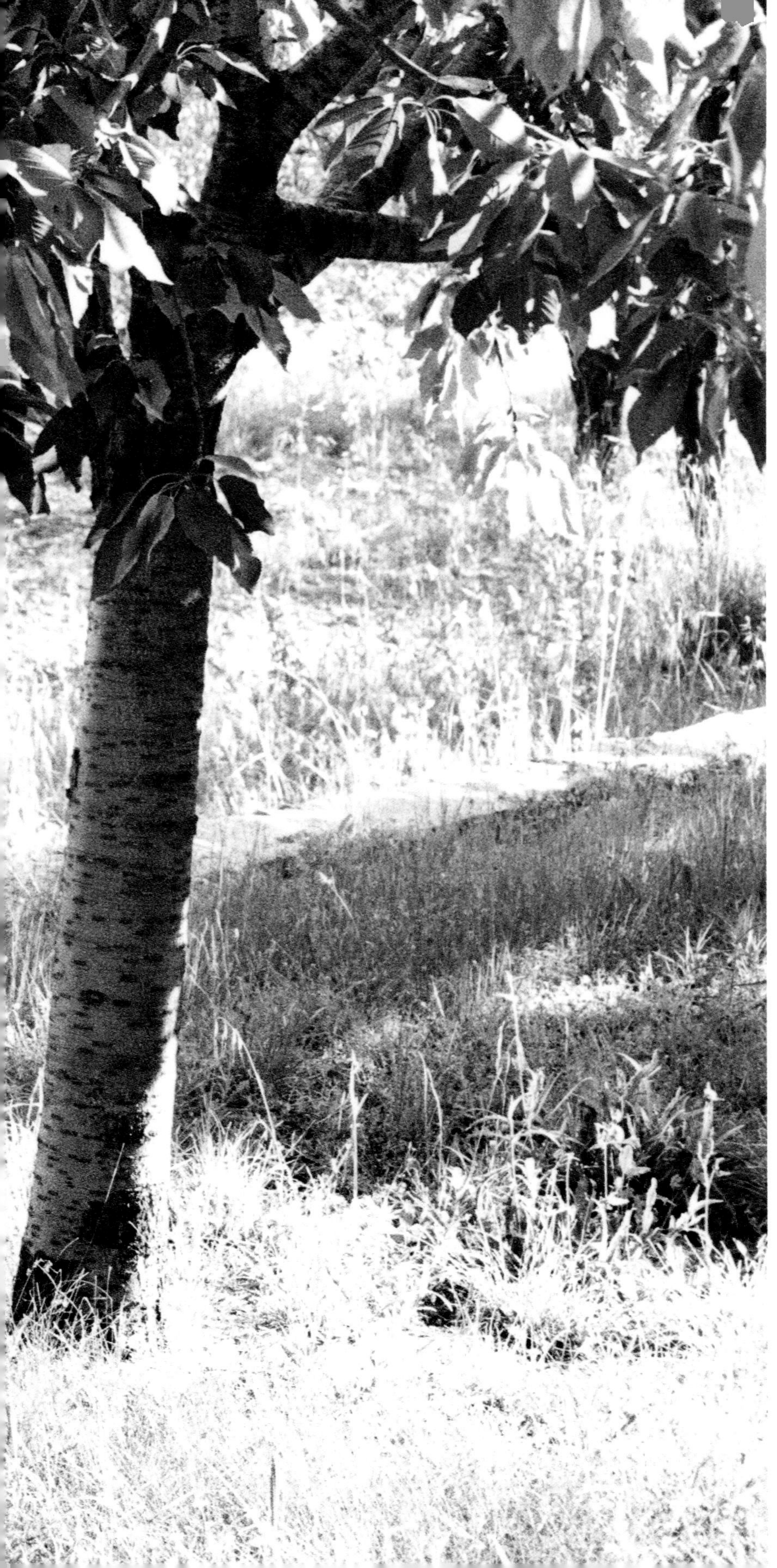

Four arms. Four legs.
One heart. One mind.
One soul. Always.

HAYDEE SCULL

FROM 'SISTERS'

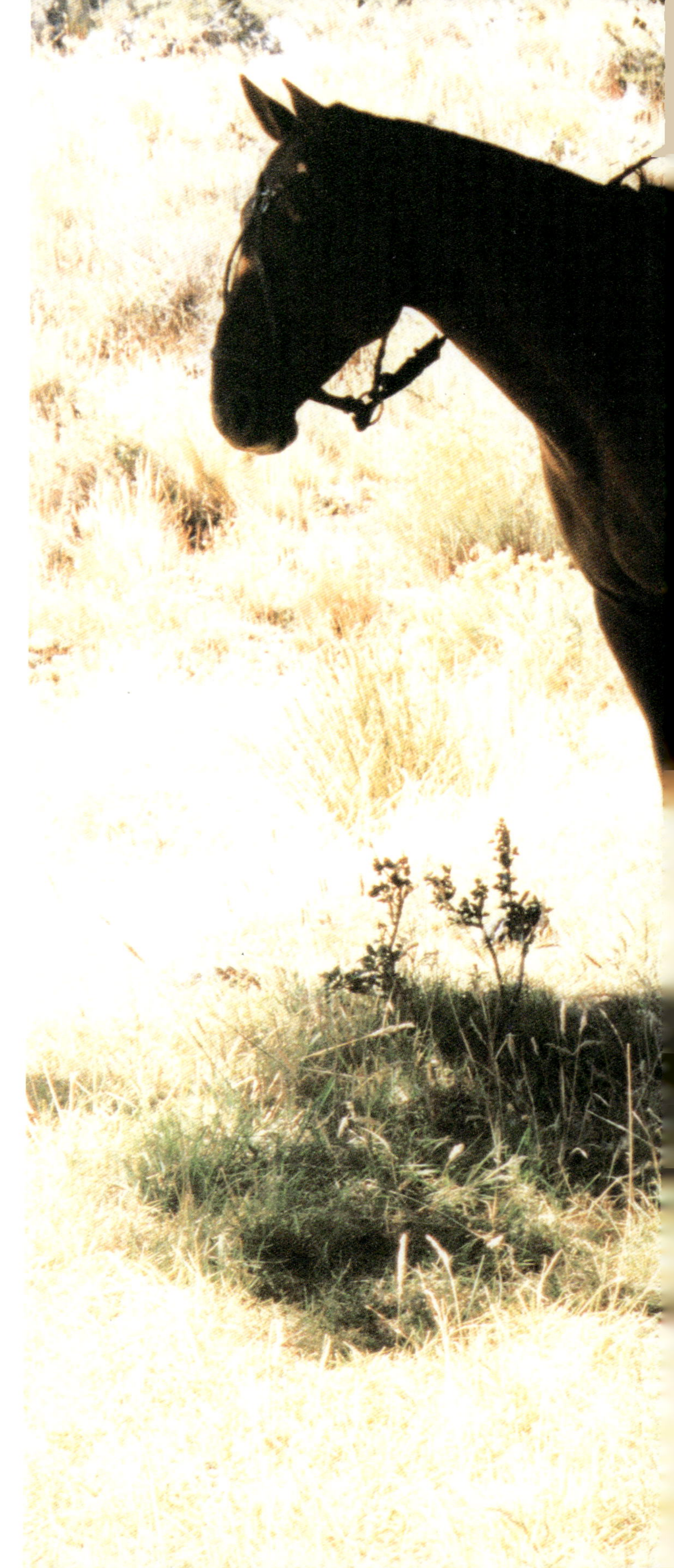

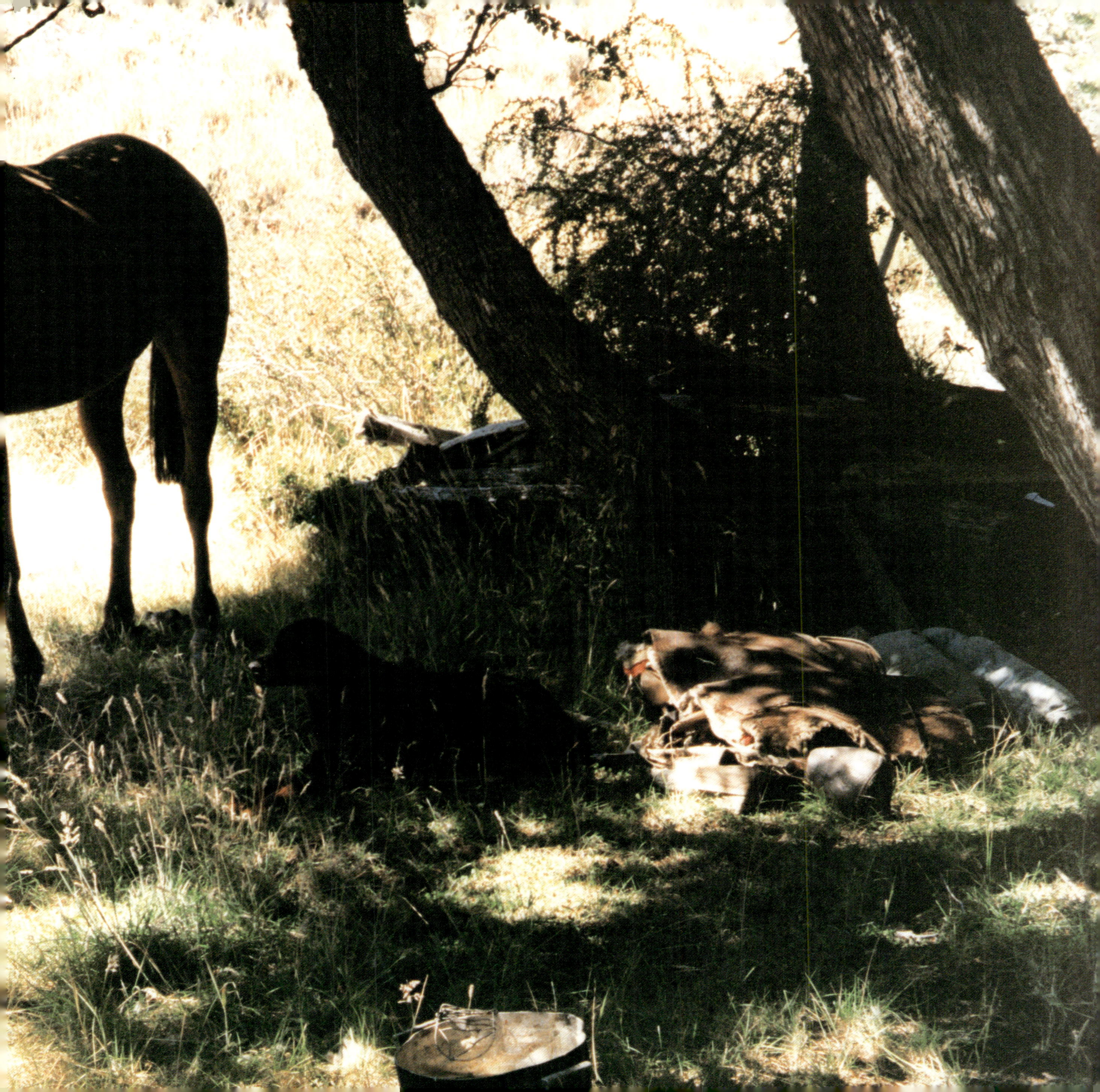

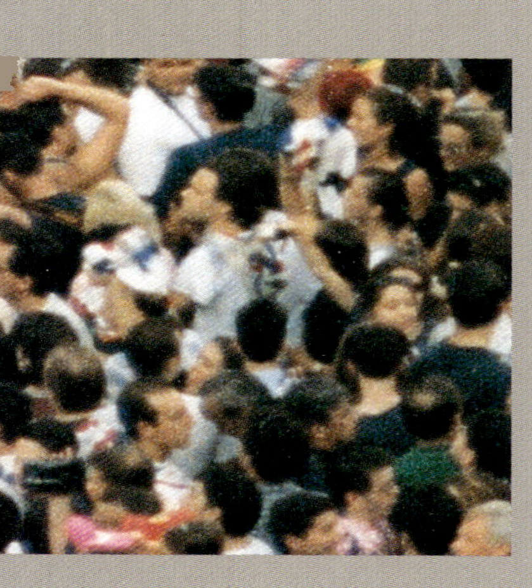

six INDIVIDUALITY

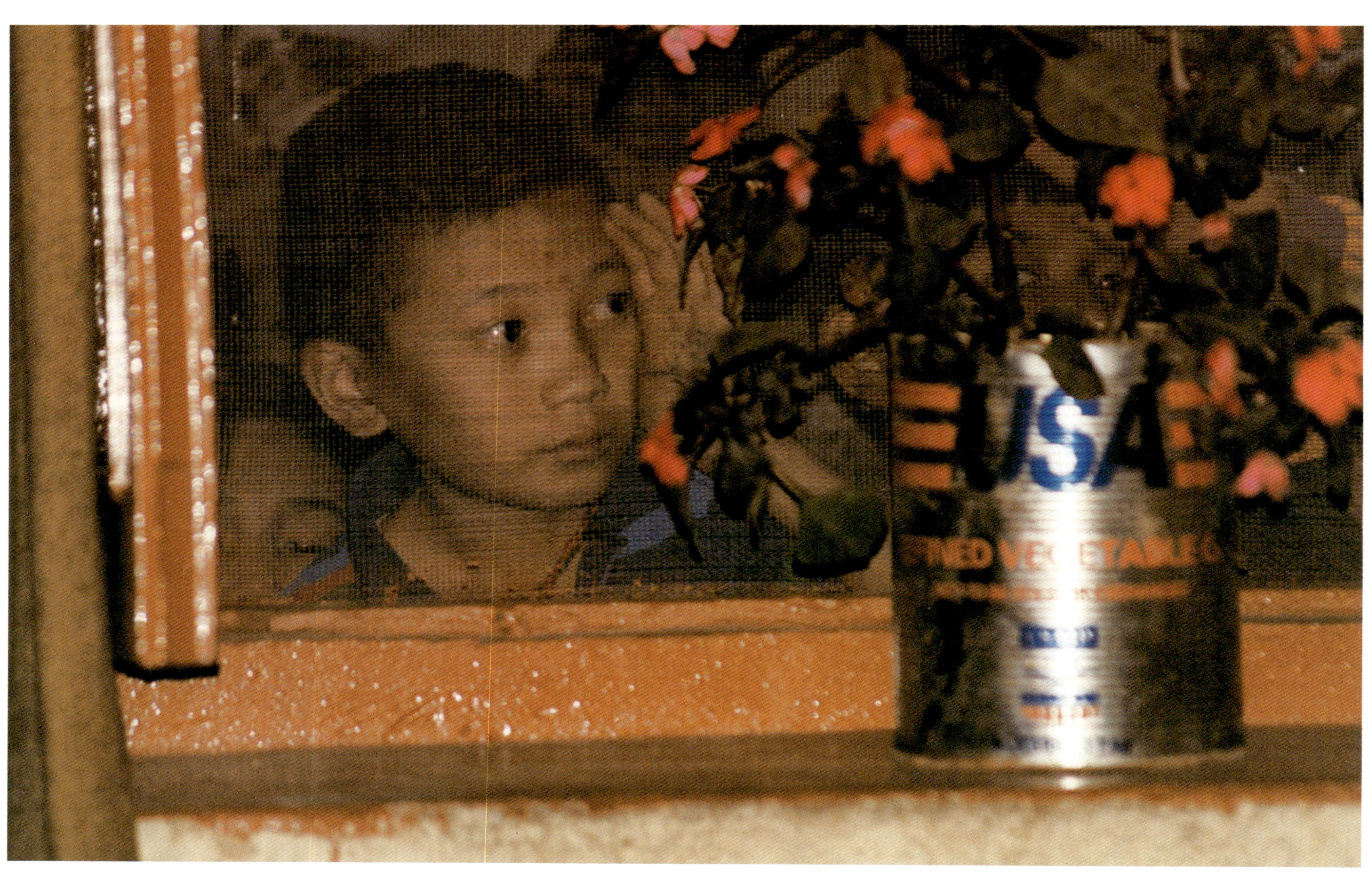
USA

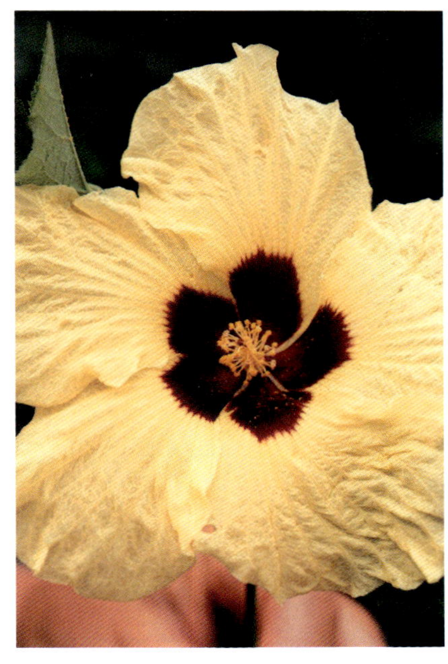

What sunshine is to flowers, smiles are to humanity.

JOSEPH ADDISON

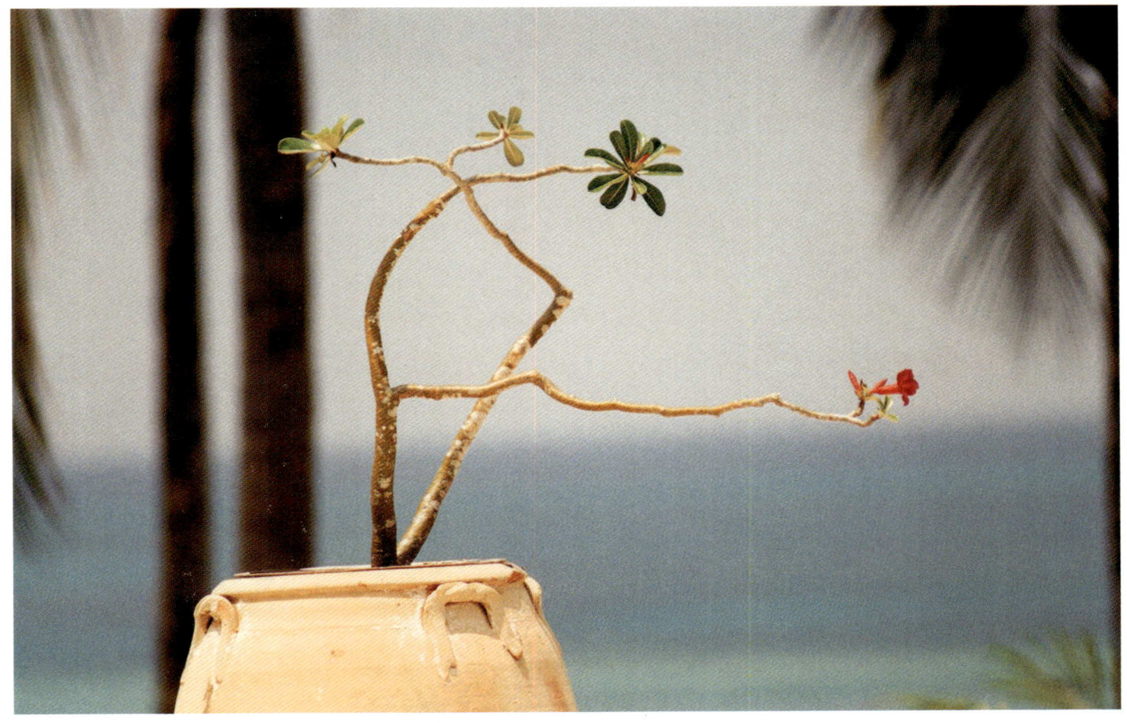

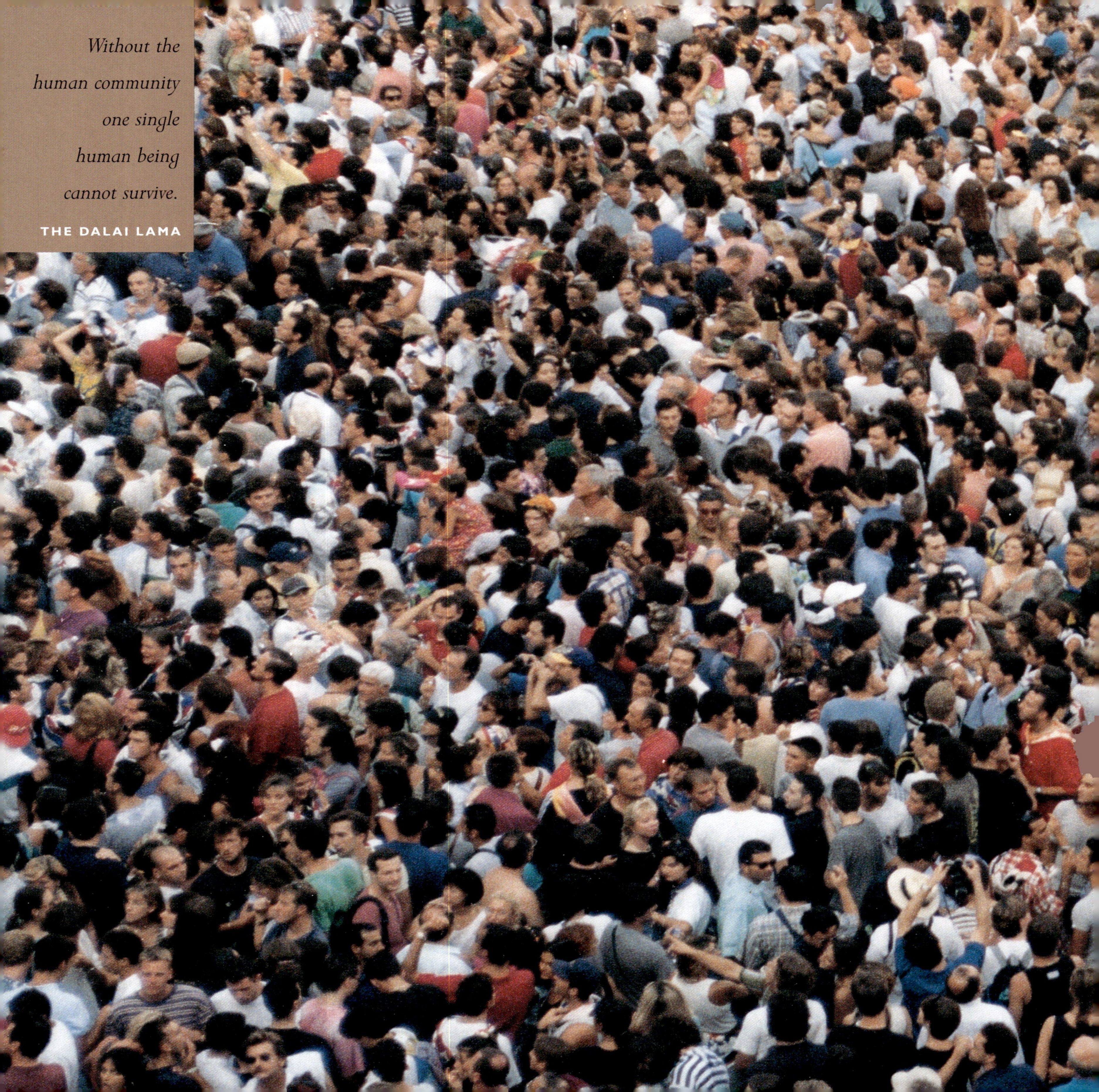

Without the human community one single human being cannot survive.

THE DALAI LAMA

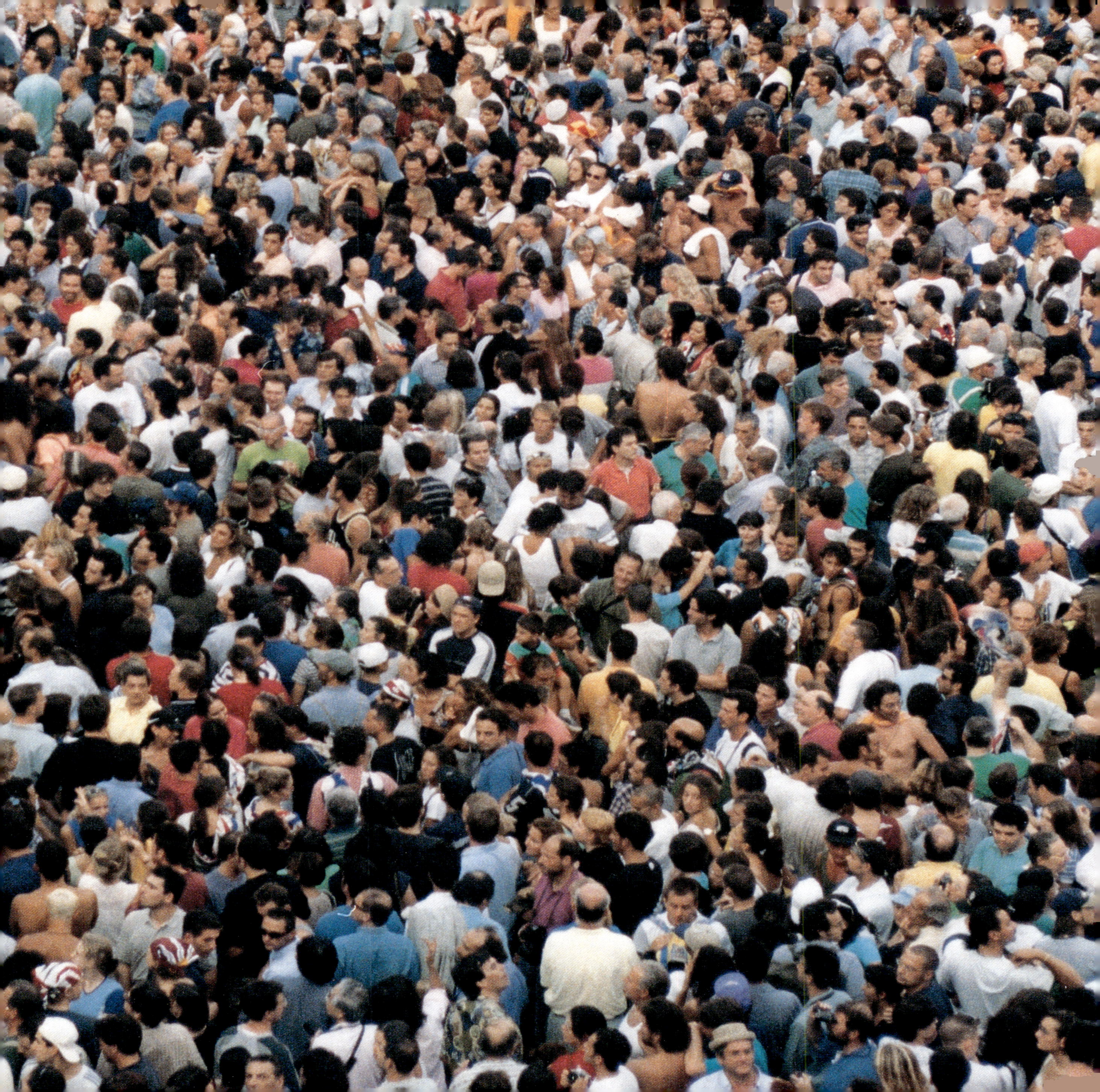

If you want others to be happy,

PRACTISE COMPASSION

If you want to be happy,

PRACTISE COMPASSION

THE DALAI LAMA

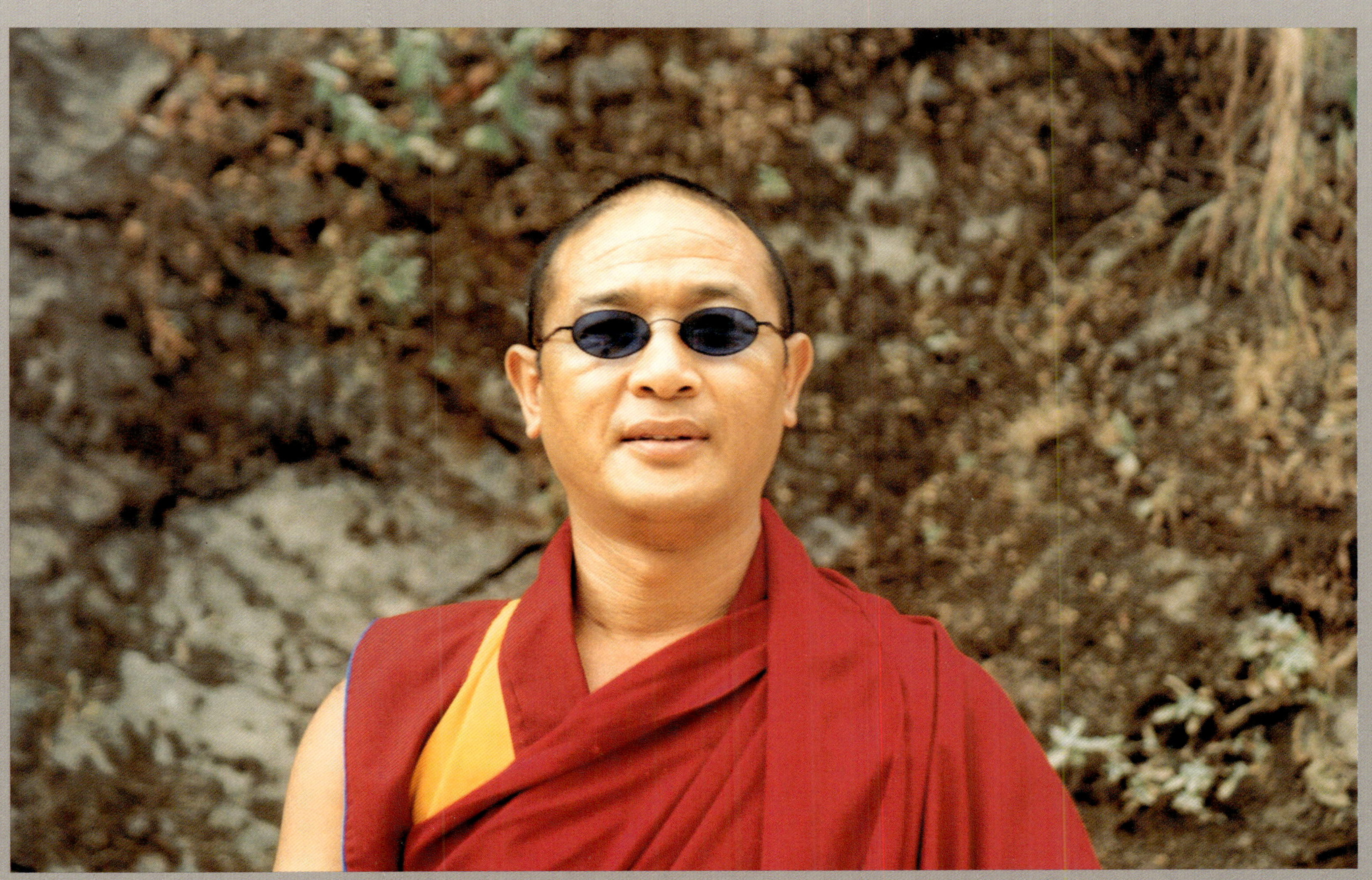

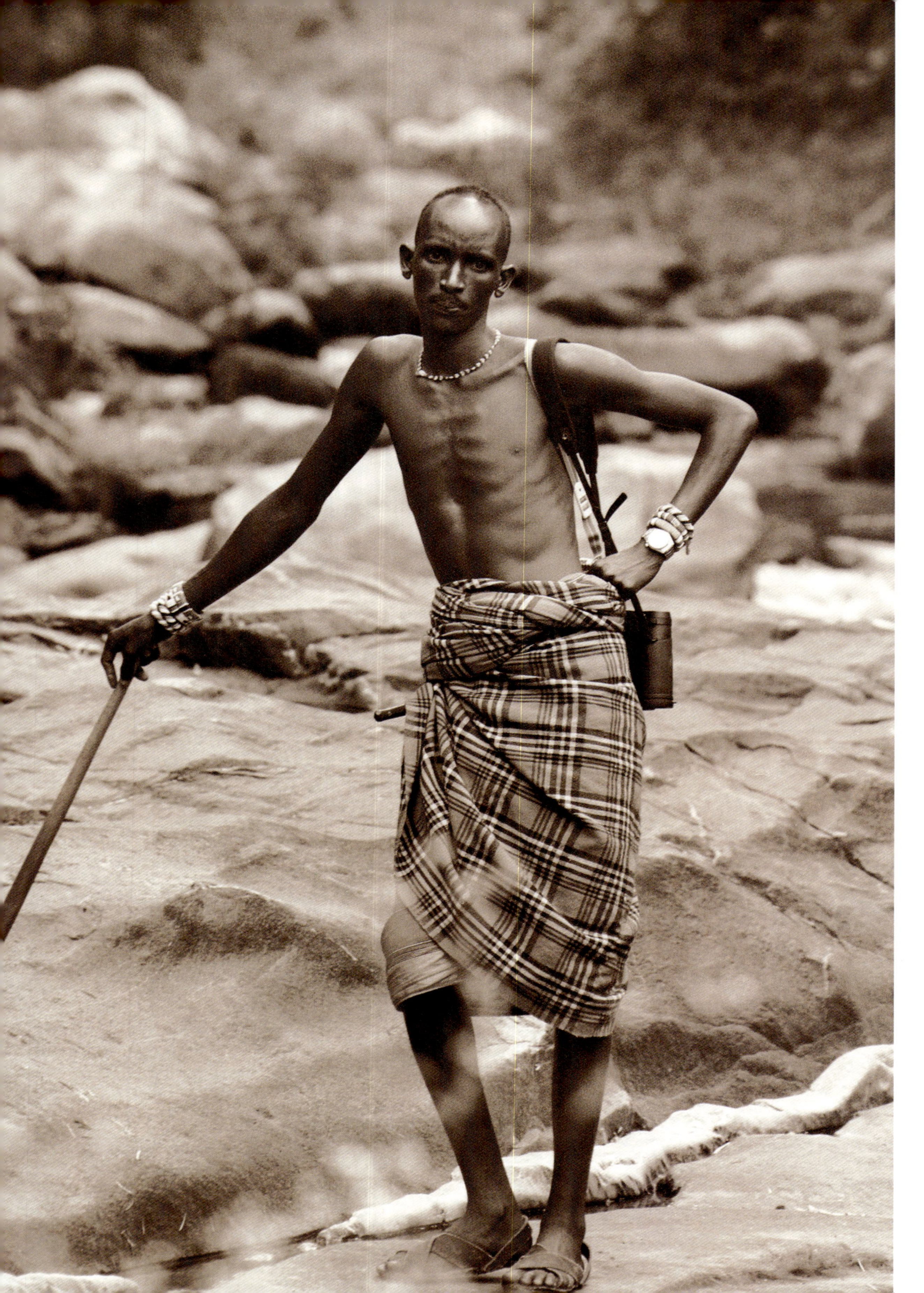

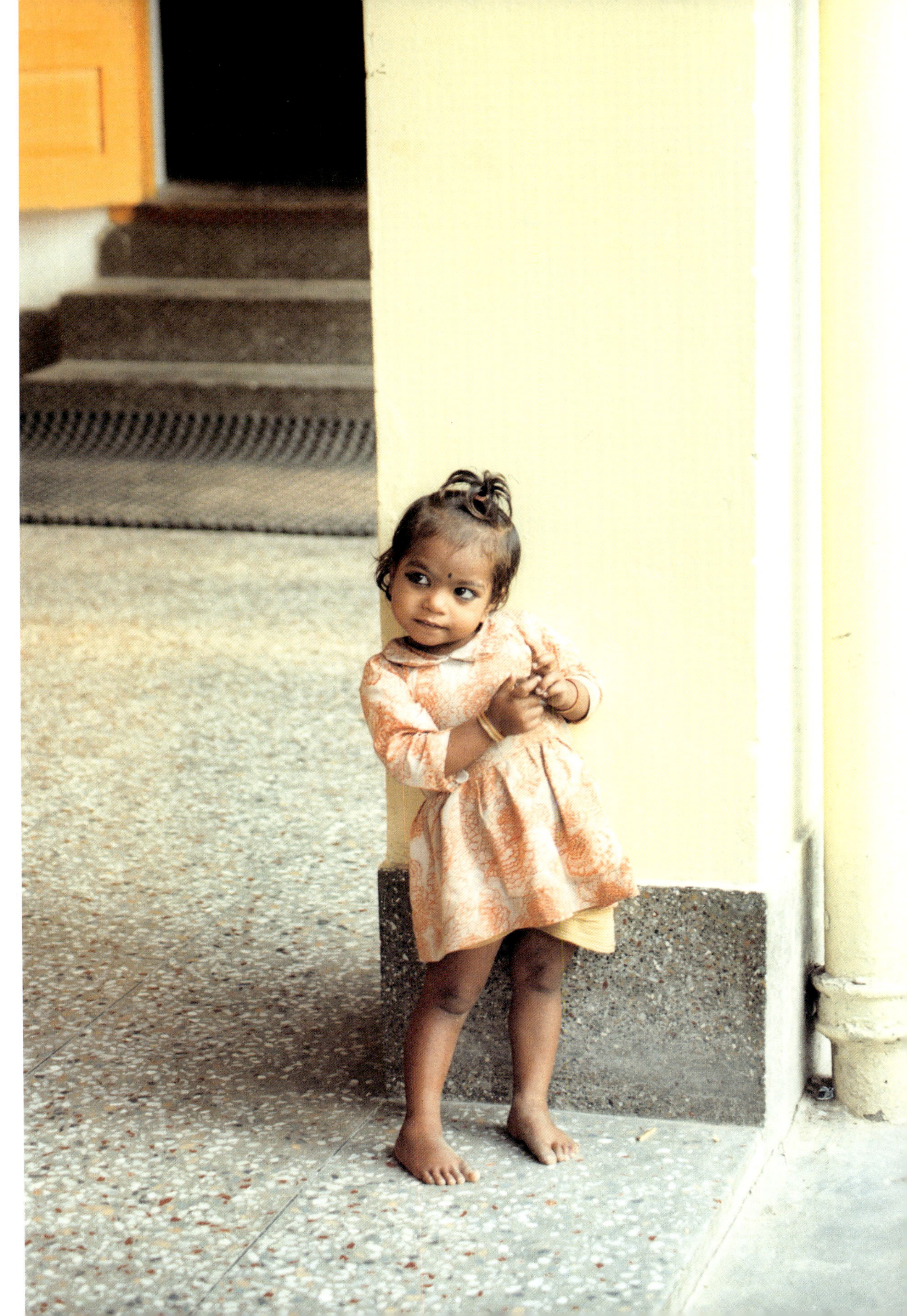

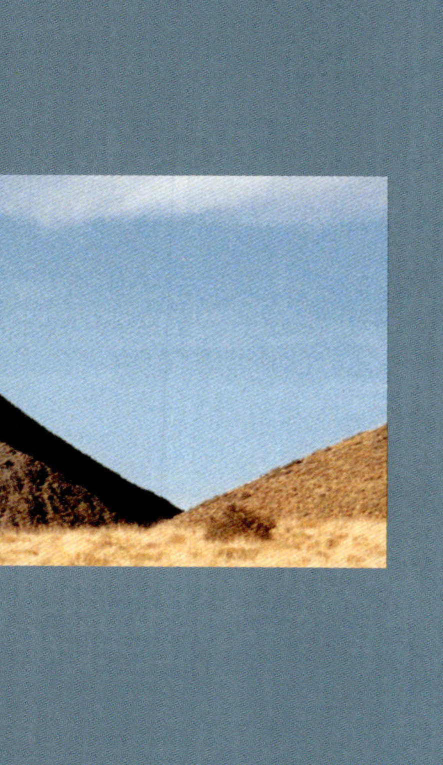

seven MOMENTS

The supreme happiness of life
is the conviction that we are
loved.

VICTOR HUGO

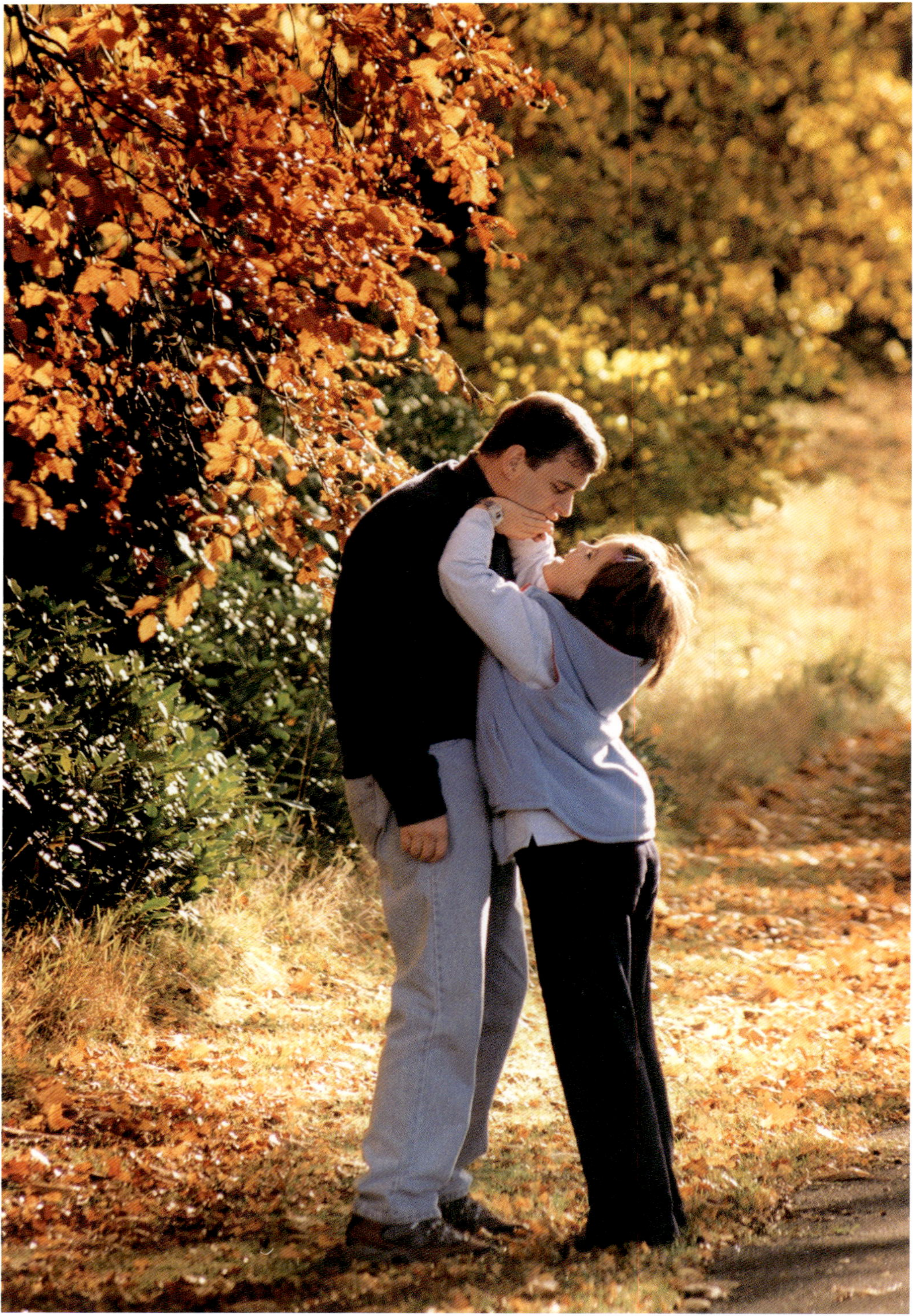

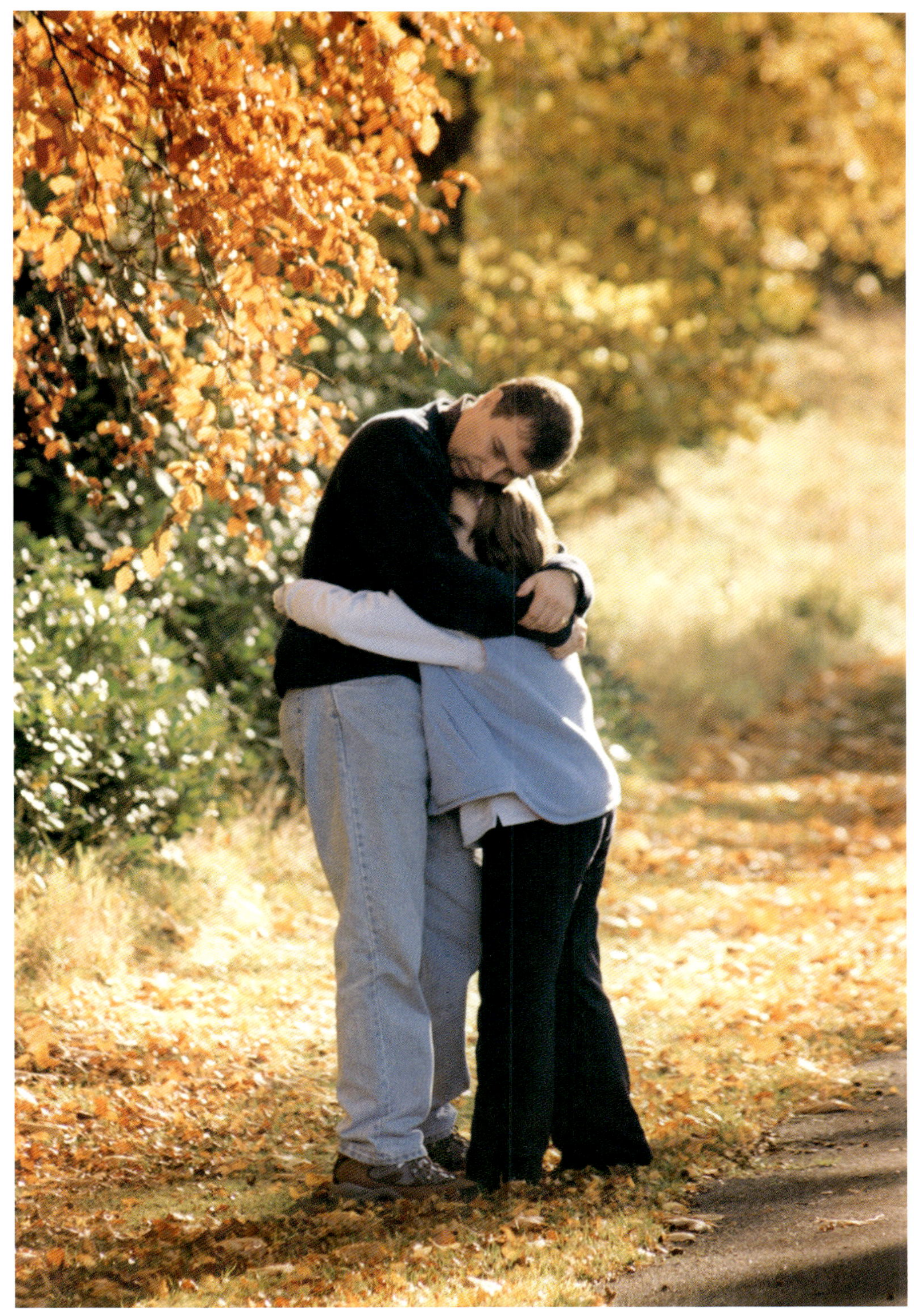

There is a silence into which
the world cannot intrude.
There is an ancient peace
you carry in your heart
and have not lost.

ANONYMOUS

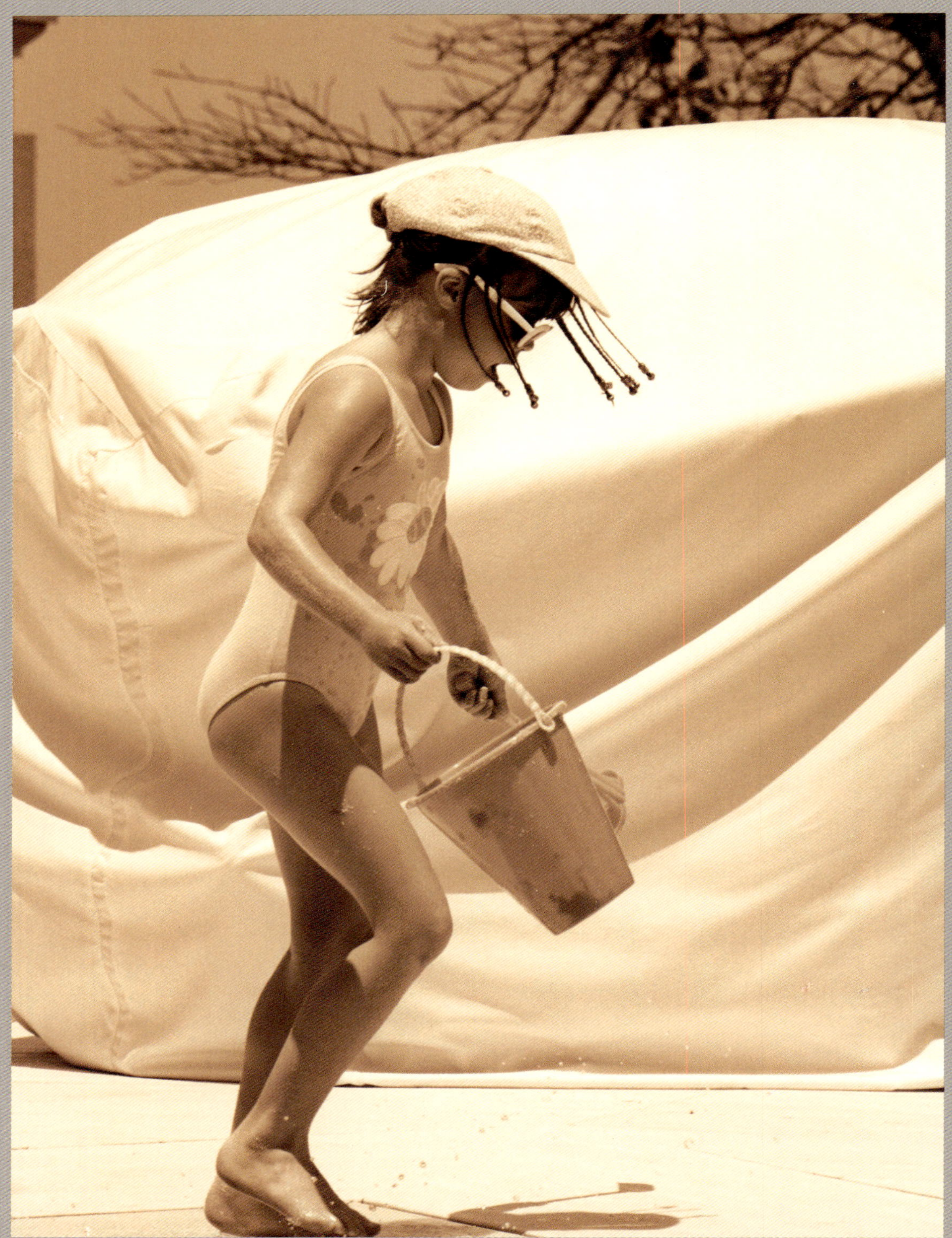

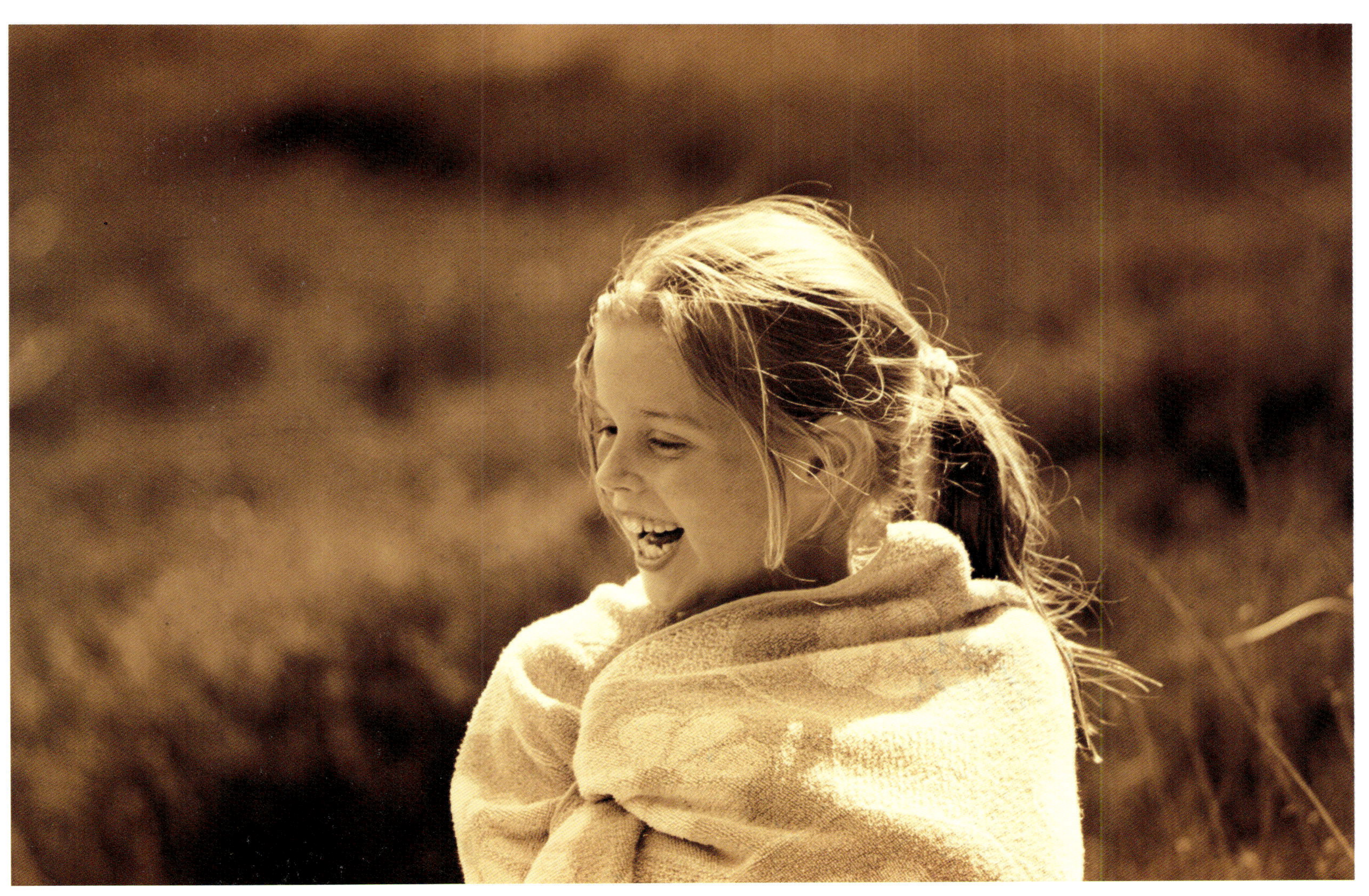

One must have chaos in oneself
in order to give birth to a dancing star.

FRIEDRICH NIETZSCHE

It began in mystery,
and it will end in mystery,
but what a savage and
beautiful country lies
in between.

DIANE ACKERMAN

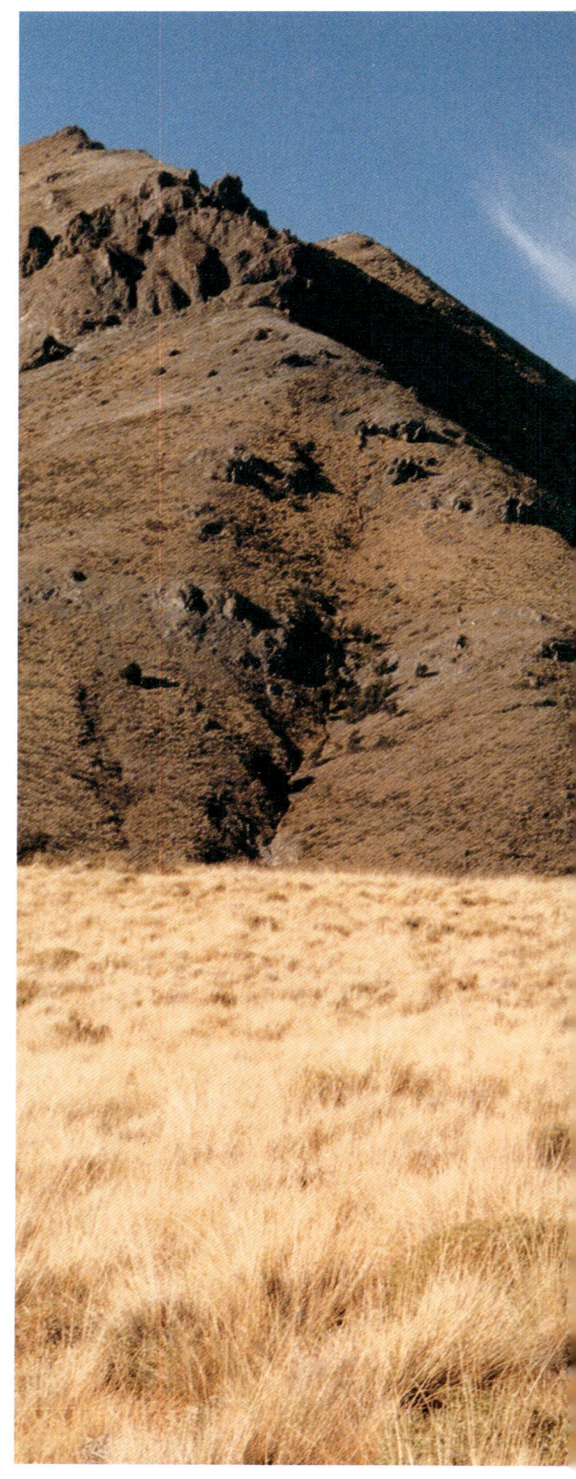

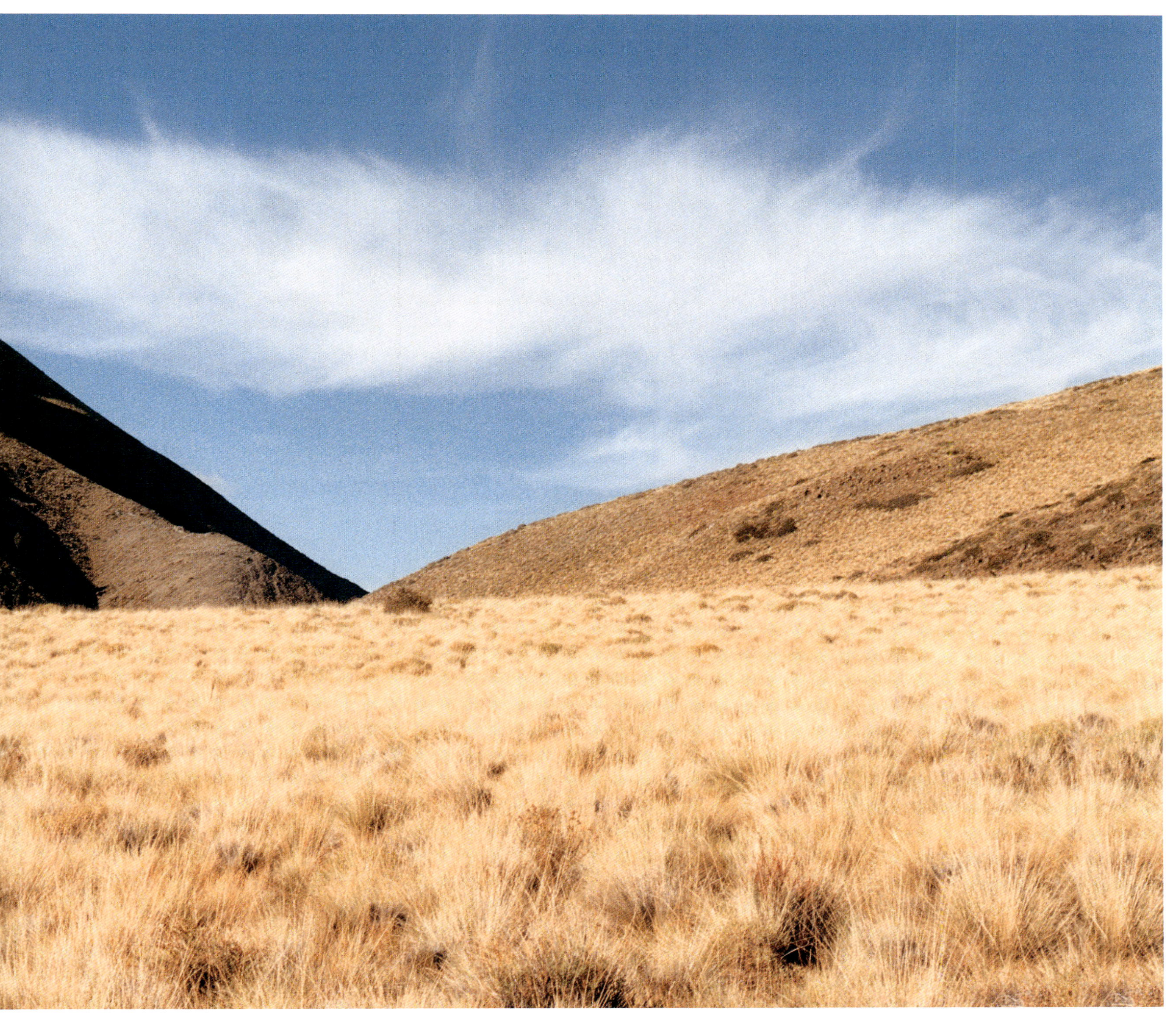

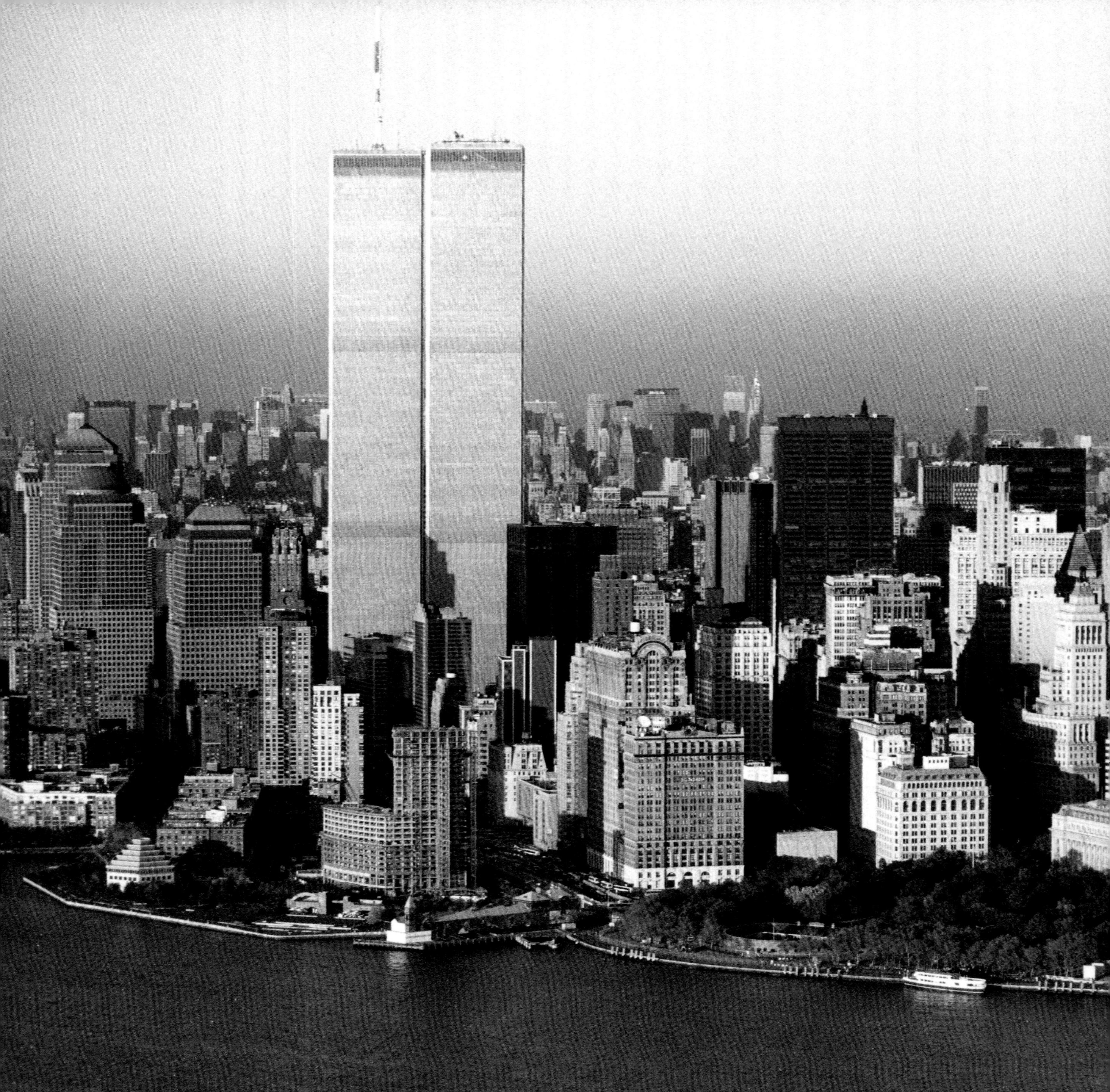

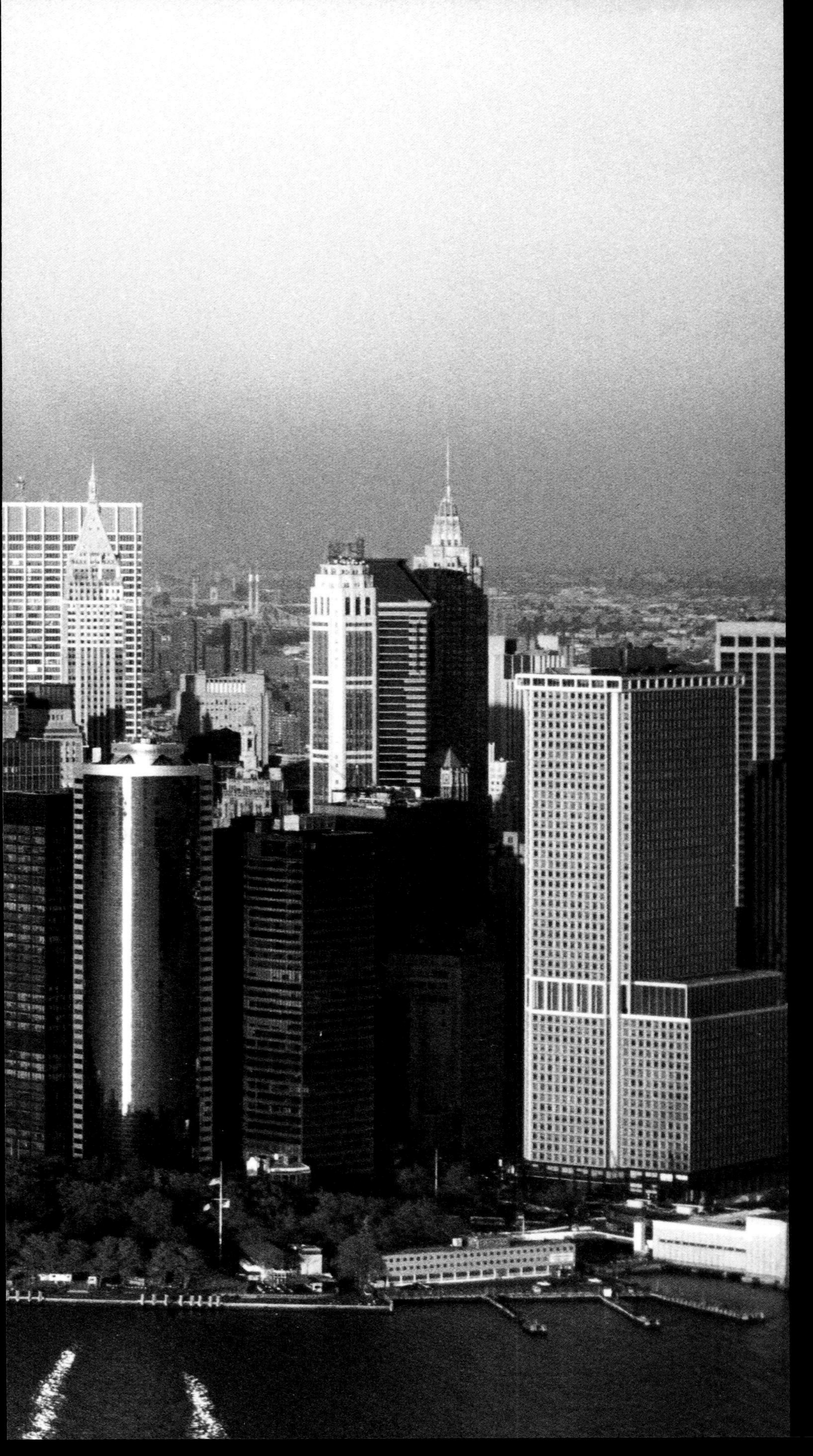

We have always held to the hope,
the belief, the conviction that there
is a better life, a better world,
beyond the horizon.

FRANKLIN DELANO ROOSEVELT

THE PICTURES

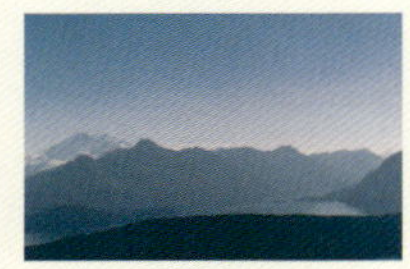

Front endpaper **BARILOCHE, ARGENTINA** *1998*
My Mum was so right when she wanted to show me her adopted country – she said that I was never to take her away from Argentina.

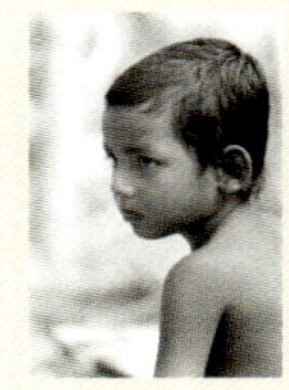

Title page **FLOODLANDS, BISHNUPUR, INDIA**
It is hard to imagine what life has in store for this orphaned child who lost his parents in the floods.

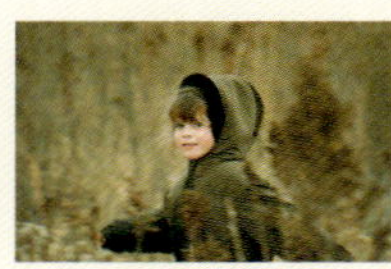

Contents page **NEW YORK** *2000*
Every day is filled with endless horizons.

Page 10 **EUGENIE, NORFOLK** *1997*
The innocent flight of youth.

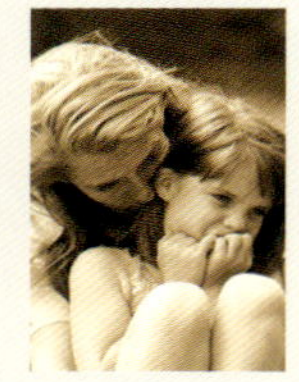

Page 15 **MUM AND EUGENIE, SCOTLAND** *1997*
Mum cherished Eugenie's every mischievous moment – in Eugenie, I think, she saw herself when she was a child.

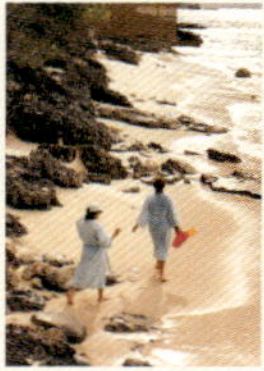

Page 16–17 **THE BAHAMAS** *2000*
Granny may live in a castle but my girls love building them!

Page 18 **DHARAMSALA, INDIA** *2000*
Ancient prayer wheels on the left and the modern Internet sign on the right – contrasting communication in today's world.

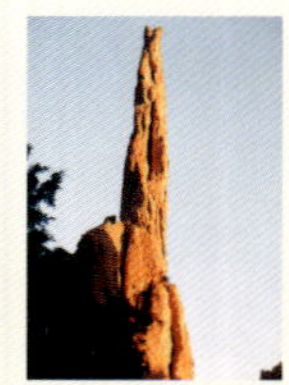

Page 19 **CATHEDRAL SPIRE, ARIZONA**
I climbed to the top of this rock with a blind mountaineer. I was terrified but he gave me the courage and determination – a truly humbling experience.

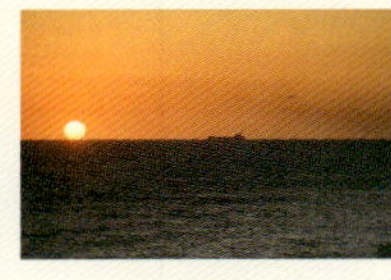

Page 20–21 **SARDINIA** *2001*
I waited and watched – appreciating the miracle of the beginning of nightfall.

Page 22 **NEW YORK** *2000*
A snapshot from a moving car.

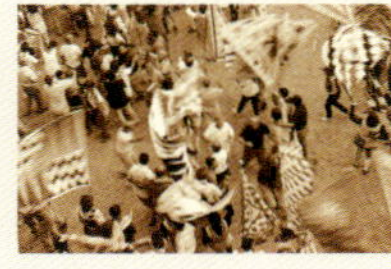

Page 24 **THE PALIO, SIENA** *1997*
History and modern life merge; a unique moment and a unique event.

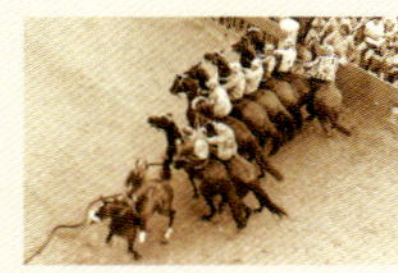

Page 25 **THE PALIO, SIENA** *1997*
The Palio: a punishing race for both horse and rider.

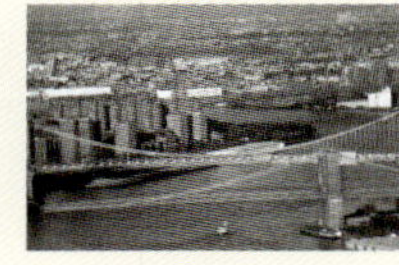

Page 28 **NEW YORK** *2000*
We move so fast in city life, and yet solitude can be found in the busiest of places.

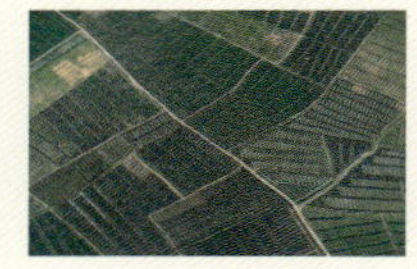

Page 30 **NEPAL** *1993*
Pure symmetry – rice fields on my way to Kathmandu.

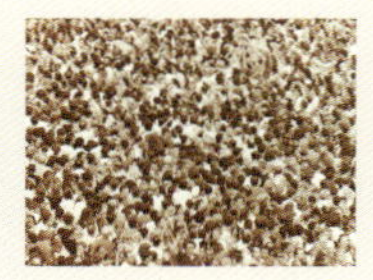

Page 32 **THE PALIO, SIENA** *1997*
A tide of humanity caught up in the frenetic atmosphere of the Palio. The race has always attracted thousands of spectators.

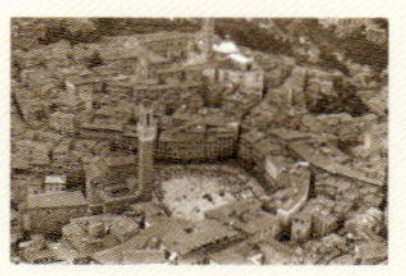

Page 33 **SIENA, ITALY** *1997*
The timeless beauty of Siena.

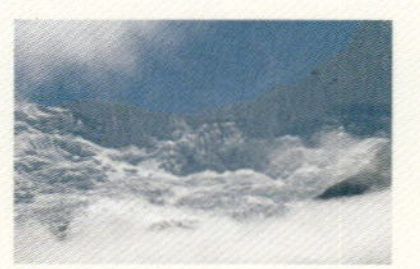

Page 34 **THE HIMALAYA** *1993*
This glacier's haunting creaks confirmed to me that Nature is alive and will win through all the abuse and destruction of our environment.

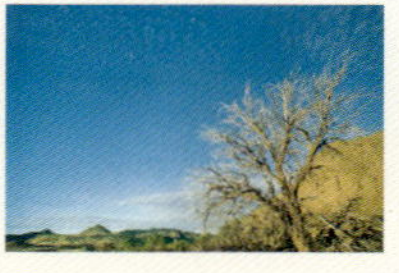

Page 36 **PATAGONIA, ARGENTINA** *2001*
This picture feeds my soul – such clarity, peace and space

Page 40 **FLOODLANDS, BISHNUPUR, INDIA** *2000*
The devastation left by the floods was completely heart-wrenching.

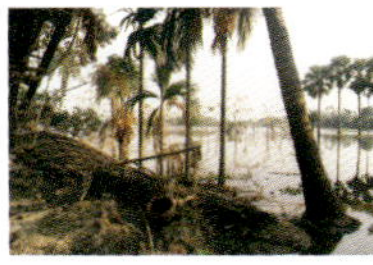

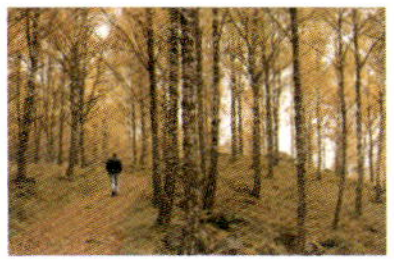

Page 42 **SCOTLAND** *2000*
Andrew loves the tranquillity and solitude of Scotland, away from the cameras – except for mine on this occasion.

Page 45 **SCOTLAND** *1999*
A sprinkle of heather and a perfect day – it can only be Scotland.

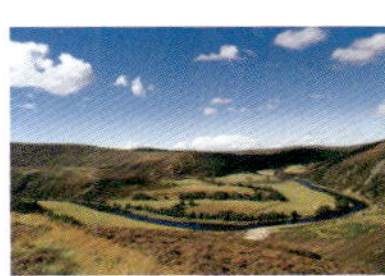

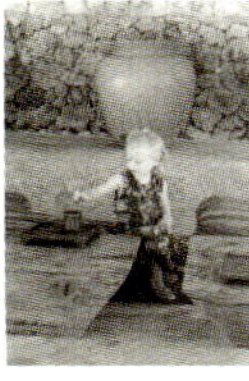

Page 47 **BEATRICE, THAILAND** *1992*
Innocence and youth: an instance captured, the magical soul of my daughter, Beatrice.

Page 50 **THE HIMALAYA** *1993*
It was cold, very cold, at Base Camp before we ascended Pokalde Peak at 19,000 feet without oxygen.

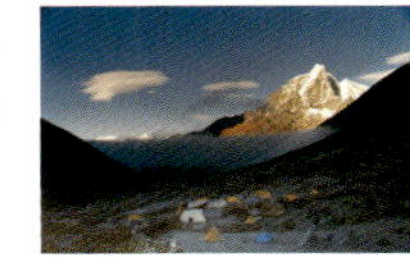

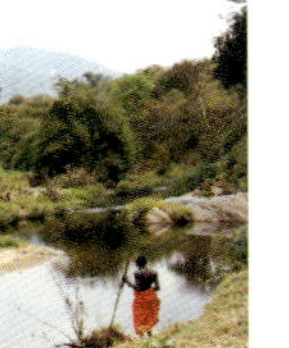

Page 52 **KENYA** *1998*
He was trying to find a way across – in the end we swam.

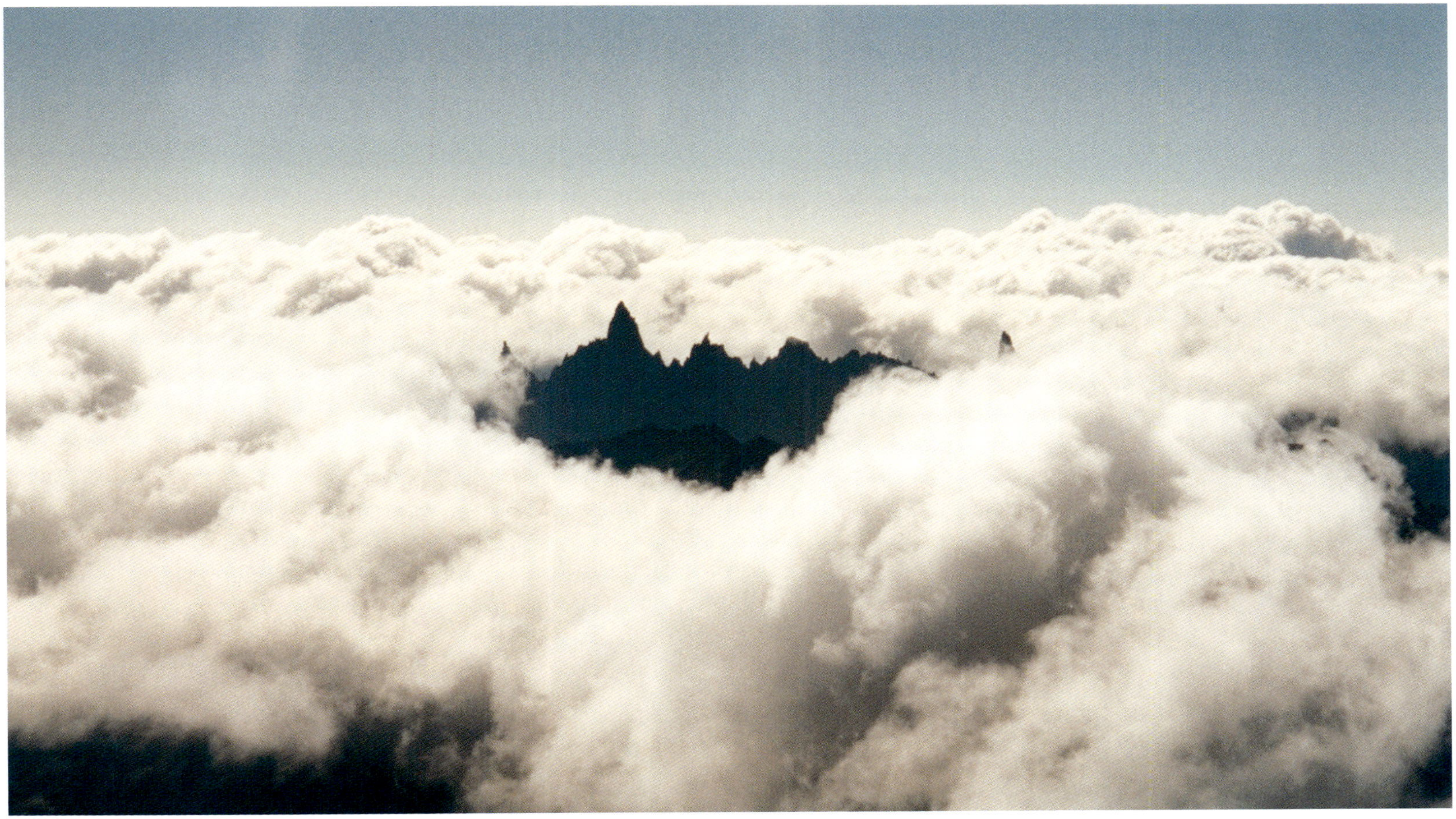

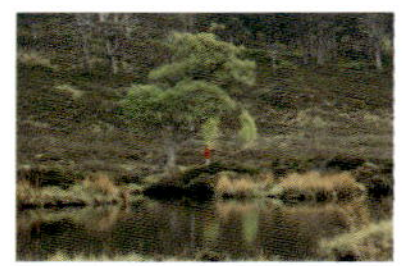

Page 53 **BEATRICE, SCOTLAND** *1997*
God's blessings: Children and nature. A brief moment in Beatrice's young life when she stood still.

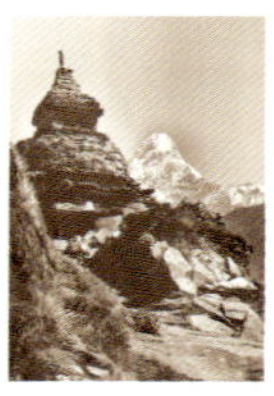

Page 54 **THE HIMALAYA** *1993*
Around every corner I saw a potential photograph or painting. The mountains are, for me, the most humbling of places.

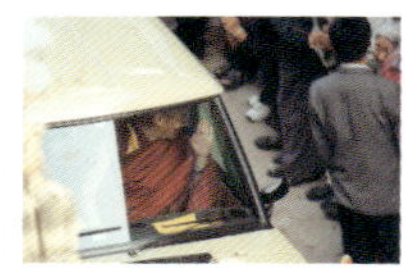

Page 56 **DHARAMSALA** *2000*
I happened to be dropped at the wrong corner by a taxi in Dharamsala – seconds later it turned out to be the right corner.

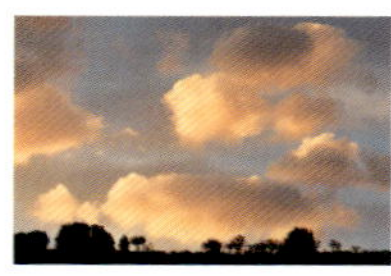

Page 60 **PATAGONIA, ARGENTINA** *1999*
It seemed as if the land had been set on fire as the sun dipped behind the Patagonian hills.

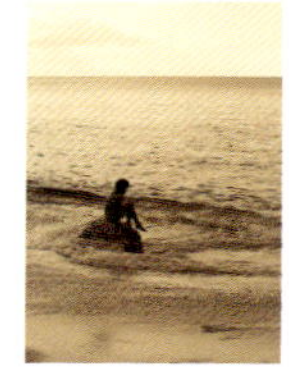

Page 63 **THE BAHAMAS** *1998*
I love the way my girls take time to feel, to see and to ponder…

Page 64 **US VIRGIN ISLANDS** *2000*
Decide, raise your sails and set your course, however long the journey may be.

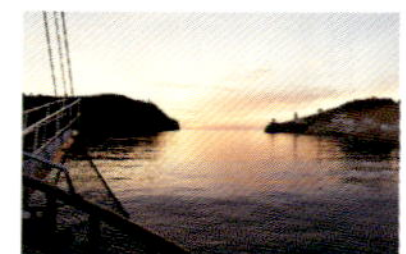

Page 67 **MAJORCA** *2000*
To reflect but not to regret. To learn and then to journey on into the great beyond.

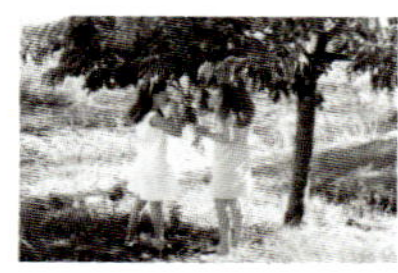

Page 68 **SEILLANS, FRANCE** *1999*
My angels…

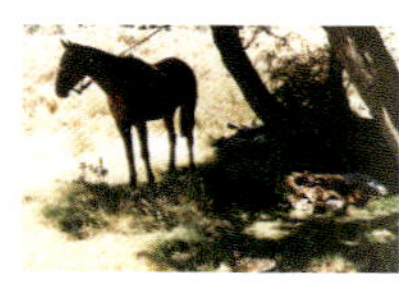

Page 70 **PATAGONIA, ARGENTINA** *1998*
A rug, a pot, a horse, a dog and a cooking pot – I took this photograph thinking how simple life could be.

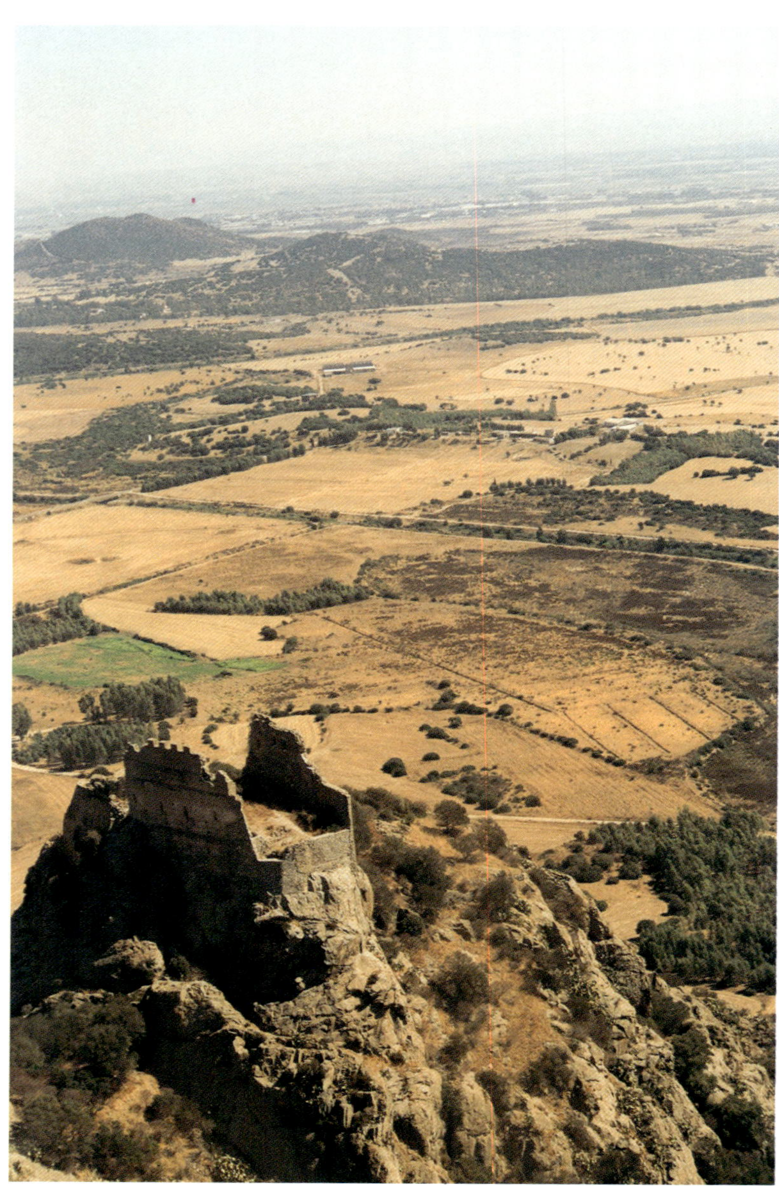

Ancient times were the youth of the world.

FRANCIS BACON

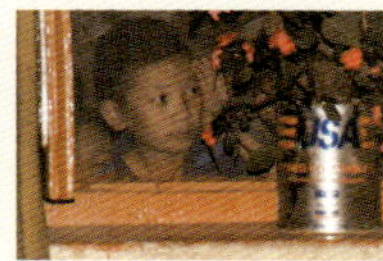

Page 74 **DHARAMSALA** *2000*
A Tibetan boy staring through the wired window of an orphanage.

Page 75 (top) **KENYA** *1998*
How can nature have created such a vision of fragility which can survive in a hostile land?

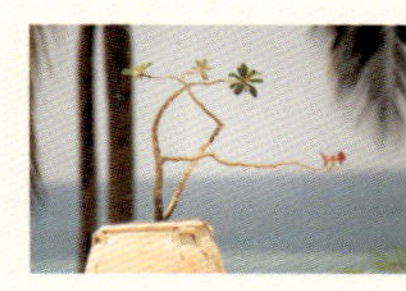

Page 75 (bottom) **THE BAHAMAS**
Nature will always win in the end. She was here before us and will be here after us – simple magic.

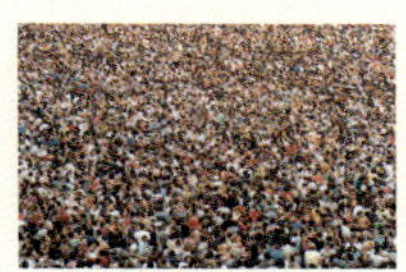

Page 76 **THE PALIO, SIENA**
A jigsaw perhaps ?! But look and think of a colour and you will find it in this scene.

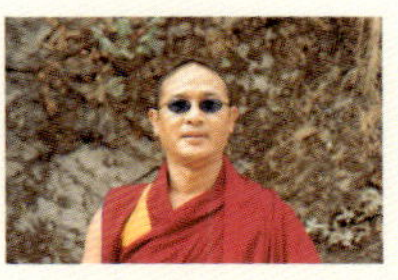

Page 79 **DHARAMSALA** *2000*
My quirky sense of humour

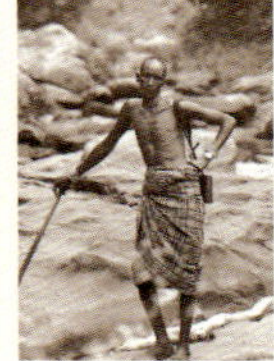

Page 80 **KENYA** *1998*
What a wonderfully natural model Ras would have made with his Burberry wrap!

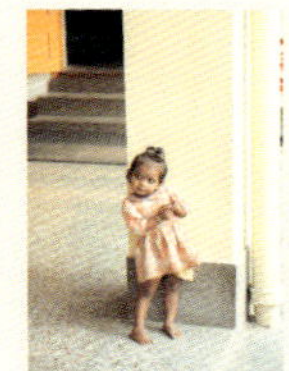

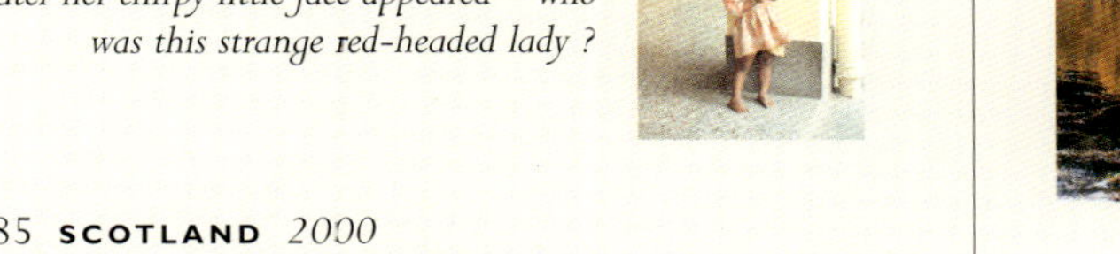

Page 81 **DHARAMSALA** *2000*
A rug was on the stone floor and this little girl was asleep underneath it. Moments later her chirpy little face appeared – who was this strange red-headed lady ?

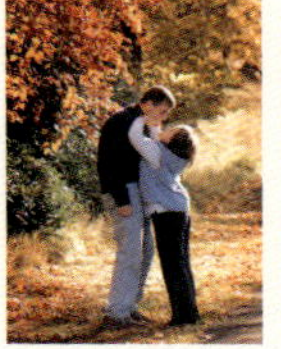

Page 84–85 **SCOTLAND** *2000*
A mother is always a rock, but from the very beginning a father's role is one which can never be replaced.

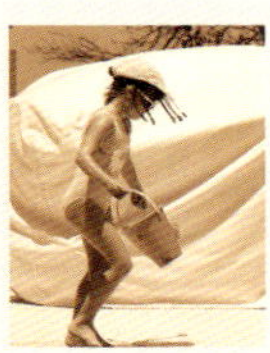

Page 86 **THE BAHAMAS** *1998*
I've absolutely no idea how I managed to get Eugenie's hair, bucket and foot all going in the same direction.

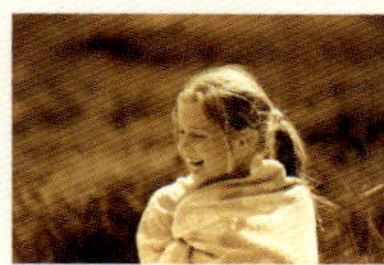

Page 87 **SCOTLAND** *1997*
An image full of laughter and joy which shows that Beatrice really lived every minute of her childhood.

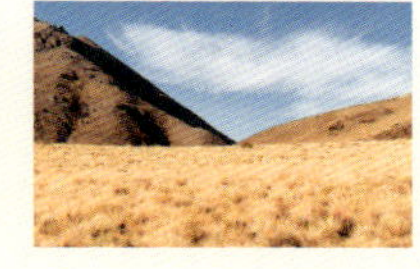

Page 88 **PATAGONIA, ARGENTINA** *1999*
I know so well how my Mum felt about her adopted country – she lived and breathed Argentina.

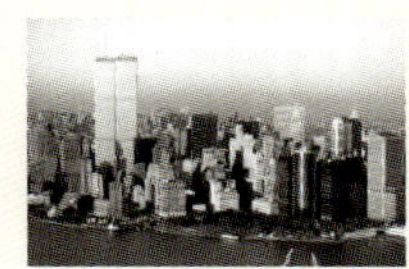

Page 90 **NEW YORK** *2000*
In memoriam…

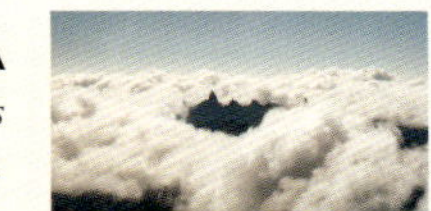

Page 93 **BARILOCHE, ARGENTINA**
I thought that this looked like a cathedral in the sky…it was taken from a helicopter in Bariloche.

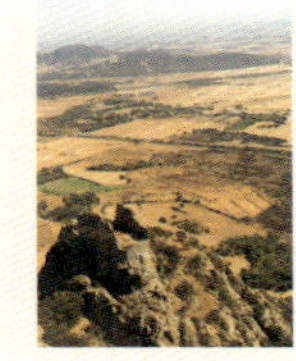

Page 94 **SARDINIA** *2001*
I think it is important to return always to our roots, to look back at history and realize our future.

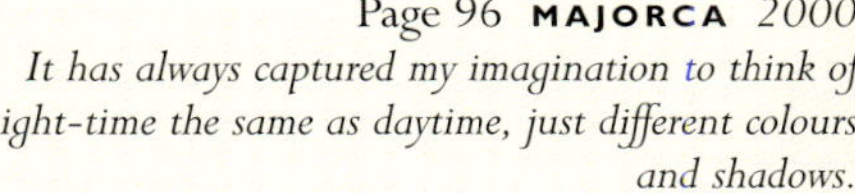

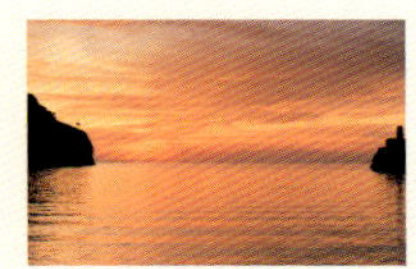

Page 96 **MAJORCA** *2000*
It has always captured my imagination to think of night-time the same as daytime, just different colours and shadows.

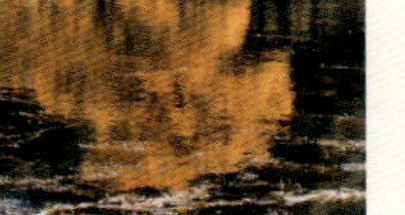

Back endpaper **SCOTLAND** *2000*
Life really is a perfect canvas on which to create your own artwork.

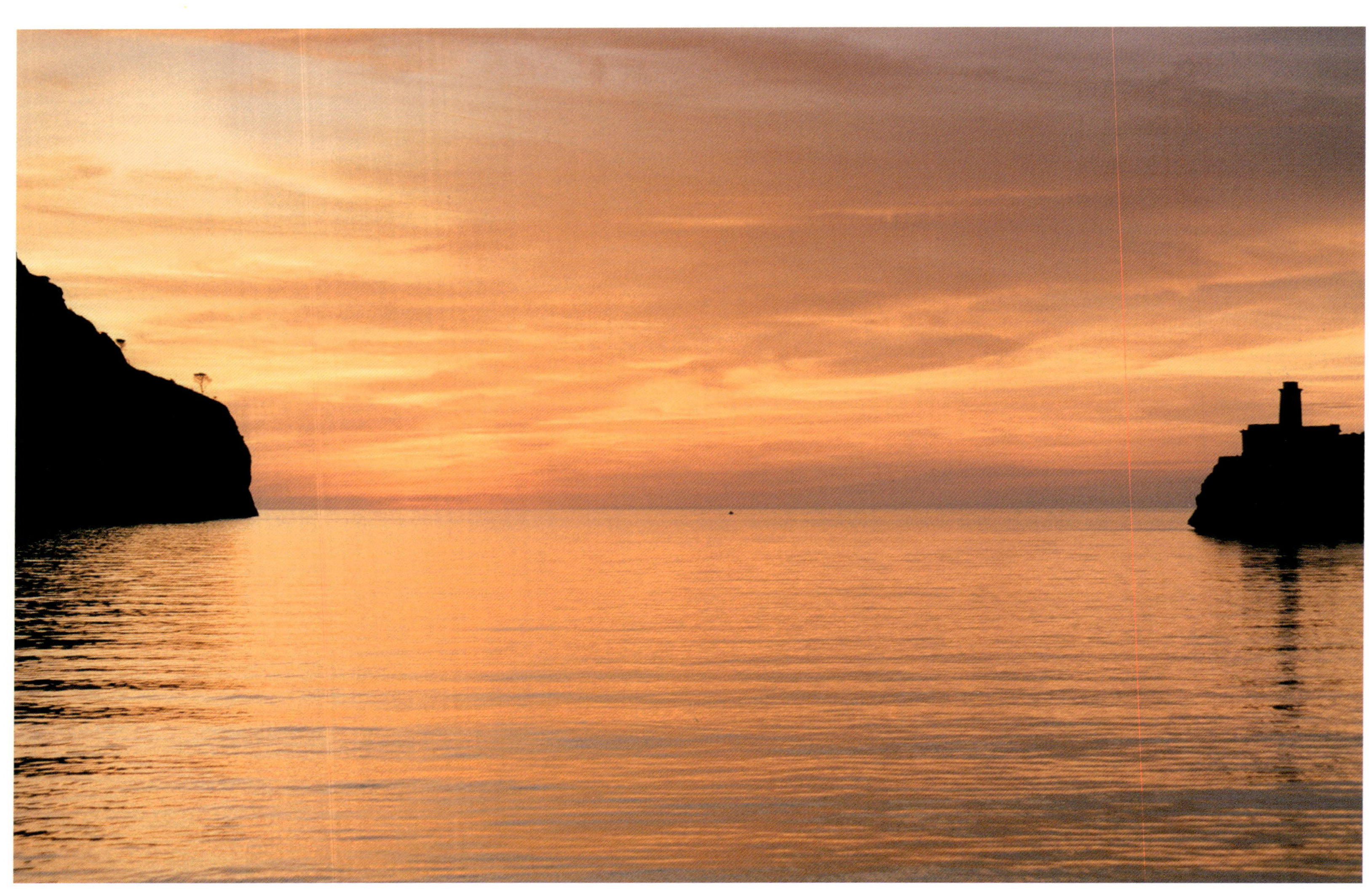

May tomorrow bring new horizons…

THE DUCHESS OF YORK

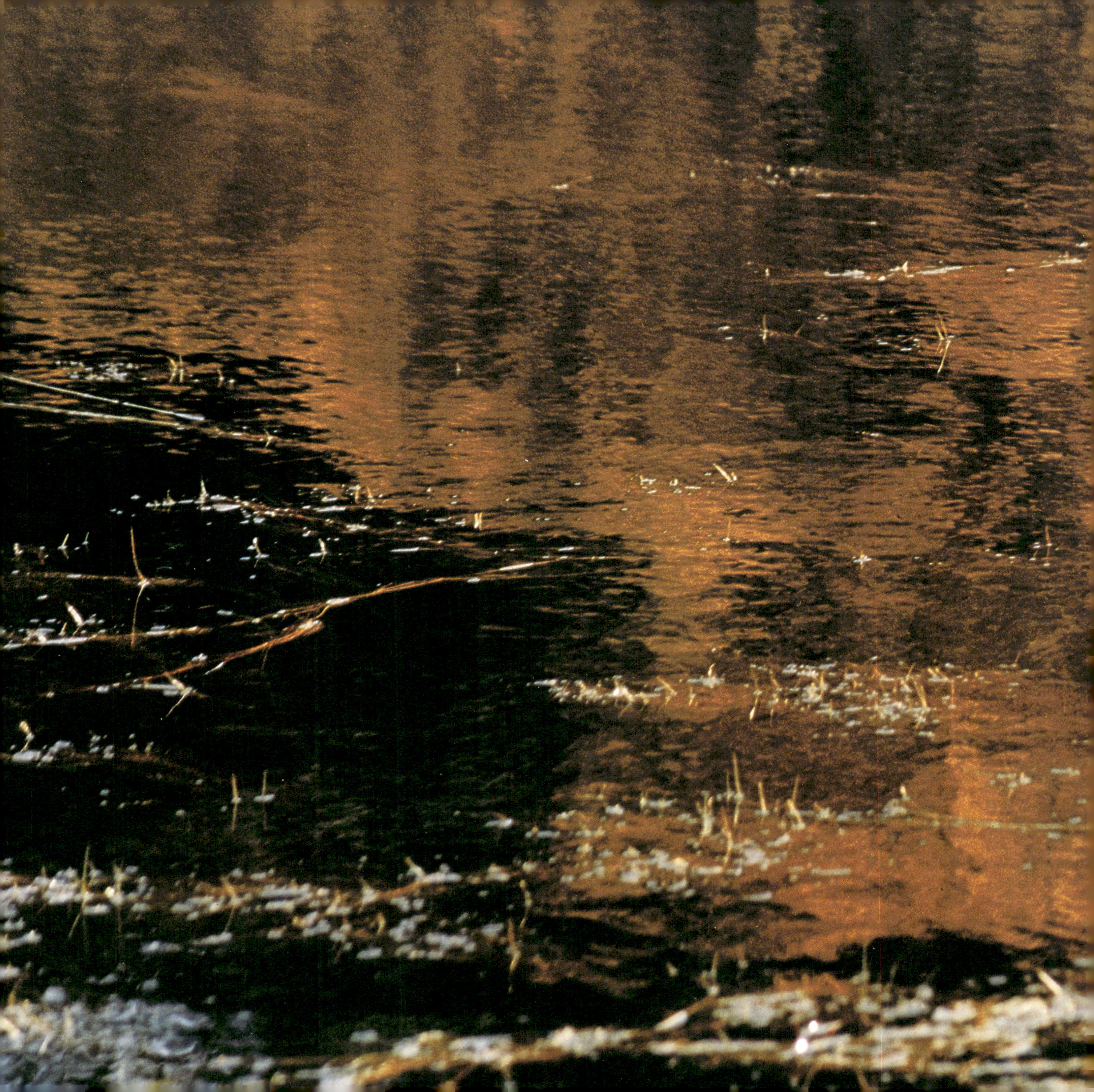